Recruit Smarter, Not Harder

Other books from HTG Press include:

Hire Tough, Manage Easy

267 Hire Tough Interview Questions

180 Ways to Build a
Magnetic Culture (with Eric Harvey)

RECRUIT SMARTER, NOT HARDER

A SIMPLE STORY THAT REVEALS
THE POWERFUL TRUTHS ABOUT
RECRUITING THE BEST HOURLY
EMPLOYEES.

MEL KLEIMAN AND BRENT KLEIMAN

Recruit Smarter, Not Harder
A story of a successful recruiter

Published by HTG Press
8300 Bissonnet, Suite 490
Houston, TX 77074
http://www.hiretough.com

Library of Congress Catalog Card Number 00-109436
ISBN 1-893214-04-4

To Sam Kleiman, in whose memory we recall the importance of dedication, devotion, and perseverance.

Acknowledgments

This book has been a collaborative effort and we give thanks to many.

Our friend Stacey Hughes deserves special mention for her contributions. Stacey took a leave from her job to join our team and apply her creative writing gift to this project.

Our longtime editor, Leslie Hamel, has again added her special touch. She gave us many helpful tips and excellent overall guidance to improve the manuscript.

We can only hope to have the opportunity to return the favor to the many friends and business associates who took the time to read the early manuscripts. Their comments and feedback were invaluable.

To our family, in particular Roberta and Debi, for believing in us, encouraging us, and always being there to give us a push in the right direction.

Foreword

The long term outlook for the economy is strong and there will be more hourly jobs than people to fill them. We forecasters who monitor economic trends expect this condition to be with us until at least 2008, maybe longer. The problem is not going away, so my advice is to change.

Change the way we do business? Not so easy. Change the way we work with our people, however, and we can put ourselves in a better position to attract and keep both customers *and* employees. Yes, it's a "people thing." But, it's not about money. If you throw more money at people without doing the other things that must be done, they'll leave anyway - muttering something like "You can't pay me enough to stay here!"

The necessary changes can't be made overnight. It takes time. And thought. And insight. And understanding coupled with action. Deliberate action.

You're about to learn how it happens, so get ready for some fascinating discoveries. Watch out, though. This delightful book is deceivingly fast moving. You'll get so caught up in the story that you'll miss some key points. You'll be tempted to think, "Oh, yeah, of course," and keep reading. Let me suggest that to get the most from this book, you read it several times.

Then comes the good part - putting the philosophy and tactics of a *Recruit Smarter*® to work in the real world. Enjoy learning, then making a difference in your organization. This book will make work fun again!

Roger E. Herman,
Strategic Business Futurist, CEO
The Herman Group
Author of **Keeping Good People,
How to Become an Employer of Choice**

Table of Contents

INTRODUCTION

This book presents a detailed framework for addressing the specific challenges of recruiting hourly employees. It spells out what you need to do in order to create what we call a *Magnetic Company*® - a company that naturally attracts, selects, and retains the best people - and repels the rest. The concept is simple, yet powerful - become the employer-of-choice among your ideal, potential employees by focusing all your resources on attracting specific types of applicants.

The impact of a concentrated recruiting effort can be illustrated by a simple analogy; when a 110-pound woman in high-heeled shoes walks across sun-heated asphalt, her heels sink into the soft surface because most of her weight is concentrated on two small points. Conversely, flat-heeled shoes, which spread her weight out evenly, won't make any impression - nor, for that matter, will a 30,000-pound steamroller.

In the same way, all of your recruiting efforts should be focused toward specific types of potential employees. Then the concentrated weight of your efforts will be directed toward precise parts of the labor pool and your results will be far more dramatic than if you used a "flat-heeled" approach (even if you spent more money on flat heels because they're more comfortable).

Instead of sending a vague, soon-to-be-forgotten message to everyone, you need to speak to your target groups directly, relevantly, and with all of your resources. One-hundred-and-ten pounds of pressure concentrated on two points create a deeper impression than 30,000 pounds spread all over.

Once you've identified your target group of applicants and communicated a positive company image with a clear strategy, you will attract more - and better - applicants than ever before.

Let's face it, your hourly employees are key to your organization's success. They're the ones who have the most customer contact. They make the sales or the products or deliver the services that make customers happy, and make them want to come back. They're also the ones who lose sales, upset customers, and cause them to go elsewhere. (One study reports 68 percent of customers who decide to take their business elsewhere do so because of an employee's attitude of indifference toward the customer.)

The bucks start here...

Stanley Marcus, chairman emeritus of Neiman-Marcus department stores, once said: "The twenty dollar bills a customer gets from the tellers in four different banks are the same. What is different are the tellers." While it's true you can get teller service from an ATM, you can only get expert service from people.

In other words, the quality of the individual providing the service is of the utmost importance. While many companies have adopted the slogan, "Our employees are our most important asset," most are achieving only inconsistent, lackluster results. Why? Because of the way they recruit, hire, and manage employees.

These employers are waiting for people who will raise their hand and "volunteer" to work for them when they should be taking an active marketing approach. In fact, most employers don't recruit at all. While they think they're recruiting by putting a sign in the front window, that old tactic just doesn't cut it any longer. The firms that are still recruiting the way they did ten or even five years ago haven't realized that if they keep doing what they've always done, they'll keep getting what they always got.

Does any business you know of hang a "Customers Wanted" sign on the door and hope for the best? Then why do so many employers depend on a "Help Wanted" sign or a single newspaper ad to recruit new hires - supposedly their most important assets?

The demand for high quality, hourly employees is forcing employers to rethink their approaches to entry-level staffing. Everyone's scrambling to find new ways to attract and retain good people, but, in the end, it all boils down to this: **To be the best, you must have the best employees. To have the best employees, you must hire the best applicants. To hire the best applicants, you must recruit the best job-seekers.**

The companies that attract a superior pool of applicants get to hire the very best people. The results are improved productivity, reduced turnover, and superior customer service. Customers like to deal with outstanding, service-minded employees. Recruiting right expands your customer base, builds customer loyalty, and increases profitability.

It's not about interviewing

There are several keys to great hiring: attracting good applicants, screening and selecting them, and keeping them. This book does not cover how to design an employment application form or conduct interviews. It does not cover how to *retain* employees - although if you hire the right people for the right jobs, you'll find that keeping them is easier than you ever imagined.

A "tough" approach to recruiting

What this book does cover is how to increase the *quantity* and the *quality* of applicants who come through your doors. It's a systematic approach to recruiting, and is, at heart, a marketing approach. This book is about how you can identify the kinds of people you want to recruit, your selling points as an employer, how to effectively target the potential employee market, and how to communicate with that market. It's definitely more work than putting an ad in the employment classifieds - and it's a lot more effective. This book is all about how to "recruit smarter" and is actually the fourth of a series.

The first title, *Hire Tough, Manage Easy: How to Find and Hire the Best Hourly Employees,* distilled the basics of an effective hiring system. Then, its companion piece, *267 Hire Tough Proven Interview Questions,* focused on the best interview questions to use to select hourly employees. Third, *180 Ways to Build a Magnetic Culture* offered you practical "How To's" for retaining the best, brightest, and most productive people.

Have some fun

This new title is not your typical business book in the tradition of "straight lecture" or case studies. We've borrowed a few experiential learning techniques and written it in novel form because it's more fun to learn when the material is entertaining or engaging.

You'll meet Scott Miller, human resources manager for Taylor's Grocery Store, a man who is becoming increasingly desperate because his recruiting efforts can't keep up with his company's rapid growth. The situation looks bleak until Scott's friend and mentor, Tom Chasen, arrives on the scene to teach him how to take a marketing approach to recruiting.

But Scott's point-of-view is only half the story. We want you to understand what the people you'd like to recruit are thinking too. Every once in a while, we'll break from Scott's story to tell you what's going on in the lives of a few of Taylor's potential applicants.

Key points are in boldface print throughout and chapter summaries outline the strategies as they develop. Finally, a summary of the Recruit Tough philosophy is presented in the appendix along with a step-by-step, tactical action plan and a comprehensive listing of recruiting resources.

CHAPTER 1:
Scott & His Dilemma

While absent-mindedly rubbing his forehead with his free hand, Scott Miller, human resources manager for Taylor's Grocery Store, thumbed through the recently submitted employment application forms he had just fished out of his overflowing in-basket. The week's collection was pathetically thin and he couldn't find a qualified candidate in the bunch. As he set the forms aside, he asked himself the question that ran through his mind at least once a day lately, "Where have all the good people gone?"

Feeling overwhelmed, Scott turned and looked out his window at the sunny, tree-lined park in the heart of Fairview City and reflected on his twelve years at Taylor's. He had joined the store as a part-time bagger during his Junior year in high school and had worked his way up through the ranks. After holding positions as stocker, checker, and assistant manager, he was promoted into the Human Resources Department.

Since Scott first joined Taylor's, Fairview City had grown to nearly 500,000 residents. And as the population had grown, so had the number of grocery stores. Intense competition was a given these days. Not only with other grocers, but with all the new fast-food franchises, restaurants, retail outlets, and entertainment venues springing up - every one of them vying for the people's time and money, as well as for the employees they all needed to deliver the goods and services.

And this was Scott's most pressing problem - employees were increasingly difficult, if not downright impossible, to find. He couldn't help but remember a time, not very long ago, when hopeful applicants turned up at the store by the dozens, and each day delivered at least one qualified person.

"And I thought I had problems then," thought Scott remorsefully. "I didn't know which applicant to choose sometimes. If only I could have that problem again."

A loud knock on his open office door jolted Scott out of his thoughts. John O'Hara, the store's general manager, walked in and slowly lowered himself into the chair opposite his HR manager. He looked tired.

"Hey, John," said Scott warily, sensing bad news. "How did your meeting with the Regional VP go?"

"Not bad, I guess, but things could certainly be better," John replied. "Sales, of course, are strong but we aren't getting much credit for that these days. The economy is such that most stores are minting money. No, what Donna Romano is all over me about our escalating employee turnover, increasing labor costs, and our customer satisfaction scores. They slipped even further last month.

"That's what I want to talk with you about, Scott. You of all people know how shorthanded we are and it's putting a strain on the whole system. But what really concerns me are the long-term implications. If our satisfaction scores are slipping, how many customers are we losing - or failing to attract in the first place?

"Strategically, we can't afford to let our service quality slip even a little. That's what Taylor's has been known for forever - that's why our customers come to us. This city is full of grocers who would love to eat away at our customer base.

"We've got to get service levels back up to their old, high standards which means we need more great people. And we've got to keep them. Think of all the money we lose when we recruit, screen, hire, and train new people, only to have them leave a few months or even a few weeks later. It's like pouring money down the drain. You've simply got to get us some great people, Scott, and fast."

"Believe me, I know," sighed Scott in frustration, "but the old days are gone. Drive around town and all you see are 'Help Wanted' and 'Now Hiring' signs, one after another. Everyone is hiring and people have their pick of any job they want."

In the tradition of battle-weary managers everywhere, John's response was pointed, "Well, get them to pick us. And they've got to be bright, service-oriented people, too. The last few you hired were practically worthless."

"I can only hire the best of who applies, you know," Scott retorted sharply.

"Then get better applicants," said John in a slightly louder voice.

Then, realizing how he must sound, John paused and regrouped. "Look, Scott, I know this labor shortage is one of your biggest headaches and I sympathize. But we have *got* to get more employees, and good ones too, or it could be the beginning of the end. Donna is not going to be patient much longer.

"I've promised her a ten percent reduction in turnover and a five percent improvement in customer-satisfaction scores by the end of the quarter. And turnover costs have to come down as well. Let me know what I can do to help - but *find us more great employees*."

As he stood and started toward the door, John had a second thought, turned, and said, "Check that - make it more *great* employees."

After John was out of sight, Scott slumped wearily over his desk and sighed while thinking: "I don't know what I'm going to do this time. I simply can't *find* great people - in fact, I can barely find *any* people at all.

"I've had 'Now Hiring' signs outside and inside the store for months, and I'm spending more and more on classified advertising. Last month, I even took twice as much ad space. I just don't know what to do next."

CHAPTER 2:
A Walk in the Park

Later that afternoon, Scott headed down the stairs for lunch. After grabbing a roast beef sandwich and soft drink from the deli, he went out and sat down on a bench on the edge of the park and tried to clear his head. There simply *had* to be a solution to his hiring problem.

While eating, Scott kept turning this dilemma over and over again in his mind. When he finished the last bite of his sandwich, he leaned back and closed his eyes. Enjoying the warm sun on his face in his peaceful part of the park, Scott slowly nodded off.

A few refreshing minutes later, Scott opened his eyes and checked his watch. When he saw he still had plenty of time, he decided to see if a walk would inspire any creative solutions. As he looked around to see which way to go, he briefly noted that something looked funny about the park. The trees seemed intensely bright, almost glowing, yet the sky was clouded over. It looked like it could rain at any moment. He had just started down his chosen path when he remembered squinting at the brightness of the blazing sun as he left Taylor's for the park earlier and thought, "Funny, no wonder weather forecasters have such a hard time getting it right."

As he emerged from the trees on the other side of the park a few minutes later, a large, modern grocery store came into view across the street. It was attractive, bright, and clean. People were streaming in and out the doors and, even from a distance, Scott could tell this was a store he would like - the energy and attractiveness of the place told him as much. He had to find out what it was all about.

As he waited for the signal to turn green, he studied the building he was approaching and thought, "Wait a minute," as he spied the logo above the automatic glass doors. "That logo - the doors - why, this is our store. How could this be? I though I was on the other side of the park. I must have been daydreaming and doubled back somehow."

And Taylor's it was, although it was easy to see how Scott could have failed to recognize it at first. The store was in better shape than he'd ever seen it and the parking lot was full. "I guess I've never used the front doors to get to my office before," Scott realized. "Things certainly look better than everyone's saying. Maybe John and Donna Romano need to see things from this angle once in a while."

As Scott moved through the parking lot, however, he couldn't shake a certain a sense of unreality. As he looked more closely, the scene seemed even more foreign. The parking lot was surprisingly clean. A cheerful, older man in a red apron was collecting the few scraps of paper and errant grocery carts that were around. Cheerful? Collecting carts? Picking up trash? Scott wondered what was going on. As he approached the red-aproned apparition, Scott half-expected him to vanish.

"Hello there," called the man, whose nametag identified him as 'Wally Thomas - Service Professional.' "Awfully nice day we're having, isn't it?" Wally continued, not waiting for a reply - which was just as well because Scott wasn't sure he could say anything anyway.

"Thanks so much for shopping at Taylor's," Wally called to a customer pulling out of the lot with her window down.

"So this *is* Taylor's," Scott said, "but who are you? You *work* here?" he asked.

"Why, of course. In fact - yes, it was you who hired me. I'm glad you did. I remember you had quite a few candidates to choose from. Taylor's sure isn't an easy place to get a job. By the way, thanks again for re-working the schedule for me. Well, I'd better be off."

The man expertly wheeled his collection of carts to the front of the store and went back inside, pausing on his way to pick up a discarded juice box.

"Well, I'll be…" murmured Scott. "Maybe I need a vacation - time for a break, perhaps - I don't remember him at all, let alone all those candidates he was talking about. But - hey, what's this?"

The two women walking toward him stopped a few feet away, behind a white, late model Buick. The one in the red apron - Scott noticed the aprons were sharper and newer than he was used to - opened the older woman's trunk and deftly loaded all the groceries.

"Thank you so much for choosing Taylor's, Mrs. Yung," the younger one said warmly.

"You know I would not shop anywhere else, Angela," the customer said with a warm smile. "There isn't a store in town that as good as yours, and the staff even knows me by name. Taylor's is Number 1 in my book."

"We love to hear that," Angela replied.

"How's school going for you?" asked Mrs. Yung. "You started at Fairview Community College, yes?"

"Oh, it's wonderful," Angela assured her. "I'm working on my degree for the next two years - and this job is perfect for that. Taylor's has been so supportive. Not only do they have a tuition reimbursement program, but they gave me time off to get my application in order, and adjusted my schedule so I could fit in all of my classes. They've assured me of a summer job, and even explained career opportunities for when I've finished."

"I think I've landed on another planet," Scott thought. "I wonder what I'll find inside - today certainly seems to be an enchanted day for Taylor's." He carefully walked through the glass doors - they were exceptionally clean - and peered cautiously around.

It was a new Taylor's, all right. The windows and aisles were cleaner than Scott had ever seen them, polished to the point of looking brand-new. Customers were smiling, and every checkout line was busy. The employees looked even happier, chatting with customers, many of whom they seemed to know well.

Baggers, checkers, and stockers were a whirl of productivity and teamwork as they transferred the groceries from counter to cart to car. Customers were moving through the lines at an astonishing pace. They didn't seem to be in such a hurry to leave, though, as they joined in the employees' conversations and jokes. Grocery shopping, typically just another chore, had been transformed into a positive experience.

"It's a positive experience for *everyone*," Scott noted. "The employees are interested and engaged, and having *fun*. And the excitement is infectious. The customers seem happier to be shopping than I've ever seen them before.

"So this must be synergy - the employees make the customers happy, and happy customers make the environment even better for the employees. The process definitely has to begin with the employees - but after that, it takes off on its own."

A few customers had gathered around to watch Mitch pack bags. (Finally, an employee Scott recognized, he noted with relief.) Mitch was practically a sideshow in himself, with his artful flourishes and remarkable pace.

"I never knew he could do that," marveled Scott.

But what was truly astounding to Scott was the number of employees on duty. He had never seen so many red aprons. It looked like Santa's workshop. And everyone was working together with so much energy. There didn't seem to be an idle employee anywhere.

As Scott looked to his right, he saw a familiar looking man striding purposefully toward him. He couldn't help but do a double take as the man's features became clear. "John?" he asked in disbelief. "Why, you're smiling. You look so happy. I hardly recognized you. How are you?"

John clapped him on the back and replied enthusiastically, "Fantastic! We're 100 percent staffed and have hopeful applicants by the dozens waiting for an opportunity here. Full- and part-time turnover rates are 50 percent below industry averages, hiring costs are down, and I've heard nothing but positive feedback from the customers. And as proof, the satisfaction scores are up 10 percent."

"That's wonderful," Scott managed in a voice that sounded quite unlike his own.

"Ever since you executed that recruiting strategy of yours, Scott, things couldn't be better. Donna is even sending out a team to interview us for the employee newsletter so she can inspire the other stores.

"Every position is filled, Scott, and we're able to take our choice of the best applicants. What a difference it has made having this caliber of people - morale is far better than it used to be, customers are having fun, and all this shows up in the numbers. The competition is dying to know our secret."

Scott himself was wondering what on earth the secret was, but was saved from commenting when, just at that moment, Donna Romano walked up and asked for a few minutes of John's time. "Wonderful job, Scott," she congratulated him. "We're going to interview you, you know, for the newsletter. I want these kinds of results in all of our stores."

After further congratulations and positive comments, the two walked away. Scott slouched back against the wall behind him, wondering how he'd failed before now to notice the employee program notices and recognition awards that filled the space to his left.

"Taylor's has become the kind of place I've always wished it could be - and somehow I'm the one getting all the credit for improved profits and everything else too. All these happy employees…and loyal customers…and applicants lining up to work here. This is just wonderful. I wonder what on earth happened?"

His question quickly became irrelevant as the wall he was leaning against began to crumble. Losing his balance, Scott toppled to the, luckily, spotless floor and landed on his back.

Then, as the room whirled, Taylor's roof opened and Scott found himself squinting up at the bright blue sky and into the face of a suited stranger who was bending over Scott, briefcase in tow, with a puzzled look on his face.

"Hey buddy, you all right?" the man asked anxiously.

Suddenly it all made sense - Scott had drifted off to sleep and fallen off the park bench. That wonderful Taylor's store - it was all just a dream.

But *what* a dream.

Filled with a burst of inspiration, Scott jumped to his feet. The stranger took a couple of cautious steps backward, but Scott took no notice. "I've had a *revelation*!" announced Scott. "A vision! And I'm the one to make it happen! I've got to get busy, busy, busy." Scott grabbed his lunch wrappings, made a three-point shot to the trashcan, and dashed off in the direction of the real Taylor's.

The suited man watched him go and then took Scott's place on the bench. Pulling his own lunch out of his briefcase, he took a bite of his sandwich and was heard to mutter, "Crazy park people."

CHAPTER 3:
A Marketing Approach to Recruiting

Back in his office, Scott sat down and reconsidered his dream in the park. A completely revitalized Taylor's. Fully staffed, applicants eager for jobs, happy and loyal customers, enhanced productivity, and a tremendous edge over the competition. And the key, Scott realized, was the people. They were happy, worked as a team, had pride in their work, and had a strong sense of what customer service really is.

Happy employees make happy customers.

"And having happy employees," reflected Scott, "means my job almost takes care of itself."

Happy customers make management happy.

"And it's a circle," Scott reflected. "Since only management can create happy employees, in this case anyway, it starts with me."

Then it quickly dawned on Scott that he had been looking at the problem from the wrong angle. "Rather than scaring up more applicants, perhaps first," he thought, "I should start to think about the good employees we already have - and how to keep them."

Keeping your good employees happy is just as important as attracting new ones.

Scott wrote his three "happiness" reminders on a sheet of paper and posted them on the wall above his desk. "Well, it seems the first step is to create happy employees. Now, I seem to remember reading something about this recently...."

Scott shuffled through the stacks of paper on his desk, then rummaged through his file cabinet. Eventually, he unearthed a dog-eared article and triumphantly pulled it out.

"Ah, ha! Here it is. Now, let's see... oh, yes, this is the right one... 'If They Don't Wanna Work for You, No One's Gonna Stop 'Em.' "

Scott scanned the article quickly for the outline of the most important elements in an employee retention strategy. First was a defined process to identify who you want to keep - to make sure it gets done; and then the five key employee motivators: growth opportunities, recognition, respect, relationships, and reward.

Outside of money, the article said those five motivators are what create sustained employee job satisfaction. In fact, growth opportunities, relationships, respect, reward, and recognition were, in the end, *more* important than pay. After all, every employer distributes paychecks, and every employee gets one. It's the "motivators" - even though they cost little or nothing - that make the difference.

People are motivated by more than just a paycheck.

The key, the article explained, is to base your strategy on the principle that *everyone is different* and, because they are, each employee responds to a different mix of motivators.

Not all employees are inspired by the same motivators.

Employees motivated by *growth opportunitie*s continuously need new things to do. They become bored easily and enjoy learning so they thrive on training. Managers should ask them regularly what they would like to do next, and what they have an interest in learning, and give them these assignments whenever possible. Most of them need to be in jobs that have promising career paths. These people need plenty of chances to prove themselves and be promoted.

Employees motivated by *recognition* find praise is what gives them the most job satisfaction. It can be delivered in private or in front of peers; it can be verbal or written, and in the form of a straightforward compliment or a fun award, but it must be genuine - people can sense and resent artificial recognition that's handed out too easily.

Those motivated by *reward* need more than just a paycheck. The best employees should always receive wages that are competitive or slightly above standard, but those motivated by reward will also need an unanticipated bonus or perk from time to time.

Every employee deserves *respect* no matter their position. This starts at the top. When management respects employees, the employees respect the customers and management as well.

Relationships are at the heart of almost every job. The relationships we develop with our peers and supervisors color every aspect of our working lives. For most people, one of the best parts about working is forming relationships with like-minded people, sharing the joys and frustrations of the job. Employers who understand the importance of relationships always do their best to select employees who fit the corporate culture.

The article went on to cover the importance of *fun* at work. No one likes to go to a place each day that's boring or stuffy or overly strict. But people do throw themselves wholeheartedly into any activity they think is fun - and that can include work.

> ***While running a business is serious, there's no reason it can't be fun.***

Scott then reviewed the reasons employees usually leave:

1) The employee did not fit the position from the start.

2) The employee was not paid enough to put up with whatever he or she had to put up with.

3) The manager didn't manage the person effectively by finding out what the employee wanted from the job - besides the taken-for-granted paycheck - and providing it.

4) Supervisors or co-workers were uncooperative, unfair, or unpleasant -

the number one reason good employees leave.

"Wow," Scott thought, "that means every time I make a hiring mistake the result could be that I lose some of the good people I've already got. As I'm figuring out what to do about recruiting, I'll do what I can to make sure we don't lose any of the good people we already have.

"But, now, back to recruiting. Even if I keep every employee I have, we're still understaffed. Our sales and profit performance are pretty good, but John is worried about our competitive position over the long term. And that will largely be determined by the quality of the people we manage to attract."

To be the best, you must hire the best.

"And since I can only hire the best of those who apply," Scott thought, "I have to recruit and attract the cream of the crop so I will have better applicants to choose from."

The best you can hire is no better than the best of those who apply.
To hire the best, you must recruit the best.

Scott couldn't get any further in this thinking that afternoon because it was time for the weekly department managers' meeting.

As soon as the meeting adjourned, Scott gathered up his papers, stuffed them in his briefcase, and left to meet his friend and mentor, Tom Chasen, for dinner.

Tom was now retired, but when Scott met him six years ago through the Fairview City Chamber of Commerce, Tom was successfully running his own citywide chain of 17 convenience stores. Among the Chamber members, Tom was known for his broad perspective and sound advice.

These days Tom taught a small business management course at the local community college and did some business consulting in his spare time. Scott often sought his advice when facing a problem or something new at Taylor's, and Tom always welcomed the opportunity to put his expertise and experience to good use.

"I'm afraid I won't be very good company this evening," Scott thought to himself. "I'm preoccupied with this hiring issue. Actually," he reconsidered, "maybe I should ask Tom about this. Surely he's faced difficult hiring situations before. I'll see what he thinks I should do."

As was their custom, the two met at the Riverview Café. As soon as they were settled in their booth, Scott launched right into what was on his mind.

"You know, Tom, I was thinking I'd ask you… how does a company get a full house of employees - and good ones at that? This job market has made it almost impossible for Taylor's to find staff, and even during times when hiring is easier, we still don't always attract the best people.

"I remember at your stores and the restaurants you managed before that you always had enough employees, and they were all attentive and service-oriented. What did you do? Did you pay a lot more than minimum wage?"

"No, not at all," Tom responded. "If I had done that, I would have gone right out of business. The economics of the convenience store and restaurant business don't support it.

"Everyone has the same problem - they need to find good people. They think they know the formula, and they follow it," Tom continued. "Most employers just put out 'Help Wanted' signs, and take out an ad in the classified section of the newspaper, right?"

Scott nodded.

"And when that doesn't work, and they still need people, and need better people, what do they do? They put out *more* signs and take out *more* ads. If it didn't work in the first place, why on earth would anyone think that doing more of the same would work any better?" Scott nodded his head as he remembered his own failed attempts with this strategy.

"After all," Tom laughed, "what's the definition of insanity?" Scott nodded his understanding as Tom answered his own question

"It's doing the exact same thing over and over again, and expecting a different result."

"If you aren't reaching the right potential employees and convincing them to come in, it's just a waste of time and money. It's throwing good money after bad. It's insane!"

Scott admitted, when Tom put it that way, he had a point.

"So, you need a new way of looking at this," announced Tom firmly. "And here it is - you need to take a *marketing approach* to recruiting."

"Marketing? What - ?"

"Listen, think about it this way. Suppose sales are off or, like always, you just want more. If you need to attract customers, how effective do you suppose it would be to hang a sign on your door that says 'Customers Wanted' or to advertise in the 'Merchandise for Sale' section of the classifieds?"

"Not very," Scott admitted.

"It's the same with employees. You have to go out and get them, and to do that you must know who they are, where they are, and what they want. It's marketing, don't you see?"

"Hmmm, I'm not sure," answered Scott.

"Well, imagine you have to come up with a product marketing strategy. What would you do?"

Scott thought for a moment. "I'd make sure my product is the best it could be, that it is priced right, and that it's something my customers want. I'd figure out who the customers are, and where they get their information, so my advertising would be in the right place at the right time.

"I'd determine what the most effective sales message would be and I'd make it easy for people to buy the product. Then, when they showed up, I'd treat them right. And then I'd keep tweaking my formula because I've learned from all the management meetings over the years that the competition changes, customers want different things, and you have to keep up."

"Exactly," agreed Tom. "Now, why do you suppose it would be any different just because the person you're trying to win over is an employee instead of a customer?"

"So the job would be my product," Scott said slowly. "It has to appeal to the right sort of employee... and I have to know who those sorts of employees are, where they are, and how to reach them.

"If my competitors have them, then I need a superior product and a superior message. And once I have them, I have to treat them right. I see what you're saying," Scott concluded.

"To be more specific," replied Tom, "Taylor's needs to become what I call a *Magnetic Company*. You need to be the one place in town where your best candidates would like to be working. When you're *magnetic*, they're naturally attracted to you as an employer.

"Understand they have choices, and most of the good people who want to work are already working. This is *always* true, regardless of the economy. However, these days, with unemployment as low as it is, the best people have more choices than ever.

"Still, you can be the one to provide the kind of responsibilities, atmosphere, training, and *fun* that edges out all the other companies who want the same people. But to do that, you have to *know* your target group."

"How difficult is that?"

"Not hard for some, impossible for others. It's just as hard as, but no harder than, attracting customers - after all, it's based on the same principles. Some companies do it with no apparent effort, while others try and try, yet just spin their wheels.

"What you've got going for you on the recruiting side is that everyone has a marketing strategy for attracting customers, but very few make a similar effort when recruiting employees.

If you put these principles into action, it gives you a real competitive advantage."

You've got to take a marketing approach to recruiting.

"The marketing approach does seem obvious, now," Scott replied. "But if it's so obvious, why *isn't everyone doing it?"*

"Everyone *says* people are their most important asset, but when it comes to making an *investment*, to putting time and money into this strategy, employers hesitate. Yes, it costs some money and time up front - but Rome wasn't built in a day. People like to see immediate results, but there's no quick answer, no free lunch, no ready-made solution."

"What's perfectly ironic, Scott, is although effective recruiting does take some up-front investment, it pays off many times over. The long-term cost-savings, enhanced teamwork and productivity, reduced turnover, and above all, customer impact, far outweigh any short-term costs.

"I've wondered myself," admitted Tom. "When we hire effectively, it's the key to sales, profits, and success, because ultimately it all comes back to people."

"I can't tell you how many studies have reached the same conclusion. They all say the companies that recruit and hire right see a significant drop in turnover as well as a rise in customer loyalty and profits.

"Besides, it's the only way to still be *around* over the long haul because the organizations that attract the best people won't just survive - they'll thrive. In my opinion, the single best use of any company's resources is to devote them to smart recruiting, hiring, and retention."

"You really feel strongly about this, don't you?" Scott asked.

"It's because I've seen too many companies - some even run by friends of mine - fail or not realize their potential only because they didn't understand this. I've also seen companies that have recognized the big picture and made this work. And, most importantly, I've done it myself, so I have firsthand evidence. But it requires commitment and energy, and a lot of managers just don't have the courage to do it."

"There's another reason, too, now that I think of it," continued Tom. "No matter how obvious it seems that a marketing approach to recruiting is the only way that works, it really is a revolutionary concept. It requires you to do more than just pay lip service to the importance of your people - you have to embrace the philosophy and live it.

"This means you put yourself - you, the manager - in the shoes of your entry-level employees. And you *think* like they do. And you care about what they care about.

"It's a whole different mindset and it makes most managers uncomfortable, but it's based on the fact that managers and employees need each other. After all, neither one has a job without the other."

"I see what you're saying," Scott replied. "It's exciting to think of what better recruiting could do for our business, but that first step does require a whole new way of thinking."

"Consider some of some of the companies that have pulled it off," Tom pointed out. "How about Southwest Airlines? You've flown them dozens of times, and everyone who has knows there's something different, something special about them.

"Southwest's management really believes that their people are their most important asset - and their actions are consistent with that belief.

The result is teamwork, productivity, and the enviable position of being one of the only consistently profitable airlines ever."

"And yet most of the other airlines have not followed suit," observed Scott.

"Exactly. It's obvious that making a commitment to people and hiring is a wise investment, and we have proof it works. But that commitment is not an easy one to make."

Tom continued, "There is hope, however. Southwest, as you know, is a relatively young company that built itself from the ground up on this philosophy.

"Many organizations don't have the luxury of starting off on the right foot. But I've seen that this mindset doesn't have to be built in from day one in order to work.

"Take Continental Airlines. For many years, they were at the bottom of the heap. When things got really bad, management finally began to rebuild their business on a foundation of respect for their employees.

"Soon, they were ranked first for customer service on long-haul flights. Their stock, as you can imagine, reflected the change as well. So you see, it's never too late."

"Well, I intend to be one of the managers who makes this happen," Scott announced. "I believe employees are Taylor's most important asset, and the single most important thing we can do is hire the best. And for that, my job is to recruit the best - and you've convinced me I can do that with your marketing approach to recruiting. I can hardly wait for this strategy to get us the results we need, Tom."

CHAPTER 3 HIGHLIGHTS

Happy employees make happy customers.

Happy customers make management happy.

Keeping your good employees happy is just as important as attracting new ones.

People are motivated by more than just a paycheck.

Not all employees are inspired by the same motivators.

While running a business is serious, there's no reason it can't be fun.

To be the best, you must hire the best. You can only hire the best of those who apply. To hire the best, you must recruit the best.

Insanity: Doing the same thing over and over again and expecting a different result!

You've got to take a marketing approach to recruiting.

CHAPTER 4:
Jobseeker Profiles

Let's take a break from Scott's story here and look at three different types of jobseekers Scott might want to recruit...

Katie: The Active Seeker

On Thursday afternoon, Katie Wilcox shifted restlessly in her chair, waiting for the last bell to ring at Lincoln High. When the jarring clangs finally began, Katie thought she'd never heard such a sweet sound in her life, and she was one of the first ones out the door.

"Wish it was Friday," her friend Becky muttered, as they tried to shove all of their books into already-crammed lockers. "What are you up to this weekend?"

Katie wrinkled her nose. "I've got to work tonight and Sunday too, unfortunately. But I'll *definitely* be at the game tomorrow night."

"You keep saying you're going to quit," replied Becky. "When?"

"I'm going to soon, Becky, but I have to find another job first. My mom insists I'm old enough to have a job, so I don't get an allowance anymore. And you know me and clothes, so I *definitely* need the cash."

The two walked down the crowded corridor, shouting in order to hear one another over the din. The two sixteen-year-olds had known each other since the fifth grade and, like most good friends, they had a lot in common - a passionate love of movies, music, chocolate, and shopping. And both girls held part-time jobs in order to earn the extra cash needed to indulge their passions.

For the past five months, Katie has been working at the extremely uncool QuickBurger, a regional fast-food chain. Because it was her very first job, she agreed to begin in the back of the restaurant flipping burgers.

She'd disliked it intensely from the start. It just didn't sync with the image of the sophisticated young lady she thought of herself as being. And the smells given off by the grease, heat, and smoke meant she had to wash her hair after every shift. But since she had no other work experience, she gritted her teeth and stuck with it.

Katie did like earning her own money though, and she *definitely* liked spending it. She also liked working with the other kids; the

QuickBurger staff was made up almost entirely of Lincoln High students.

After two months in the kitchen, Katie asked to be moved to the cash register. She was a good employee, and a fast learner, and the QuickBurger manager quickly approved. Although the job itself was better, her new supervisor had a sour disposition and a permanent scowl on her face. Naturally, most of the staff took to calling her "Old Sourpuss" behind her back.

There were two things that bugged Katie even more than smelly hair and Old Sourpuss, though. First, when she was hired, she was promised lots of training and opportunities for advancement. This hadn't happened and the intelligent girl was bored.

Second, Old Sourpuss blatantly disregarded all of Katie's scheduling preferences. Katie liked the extra money from working extra hours, but only to a point. She made it clear she preferred a limit of 20 hours per week, but Old Sourpuss was routinely short-staffed and routinely slotted Katie for longer hours - occasionally up to as many as 35 a week. The longer hours meant late nights getting homework done.

In her supervisor's defense, Katie was one of the best, most conscientious and responsible employees on staff. Old Sourpuss had learned long ago to use her best people for unpleasant tasks and to cover for tardy or no-show employees because they could be counted on to do the work without complaint - that was part and parcel of why they were a cut above.

But from Katie's perspective, it was the worst of both worlds. Getting taken advantage of for being a good worker with too little responsibility or challenge. In other words, she got no bonus points for a job well done.

So, every shift found Katie paired up with Old Sourpuss and Katie intended to change *that* as soon as humanly possible.

"Life is too short," she said firmly, "to spend even a few hours a day taking orders from a grouchy supervisor who doesn't listen to my concerns."

Hourly employees are unlikely to tolerate a disagreeable situation for long.

Derrik: The Passive Seeker

Katie entered through the QuickBurger backdoor and went to the employees' restroom to change into her uniform. While on her way to her station, she passed Derrik Hanson in the hall, a good-looking and popular student at Lincoln High and one of her classmates since grade school.

Derrik was the occasional cause of Katie's extended hours, since it was not uncommon for him to show up late, with no excuse but an apologetic smile. It was a charming smile, however, and Katie was inclined to overlook his lapses.

"Oh, *hello*, Derrik," Katie beamed, as she adjusted her uniform cap to its most flattering position.

"Hi, Katie. Ready for another day spending quality time with Old Sourpuss?"

"Definitely not," muttered Katie. "How can you possibly have worked here for a year? Doesn't she just drive you up the wall?"

"Just ignore her," suggested Derrik. "I don't know why you let her get to you."

His voice dropped a notch and he looked around to make sure they were unobserved. "Are you looking around? Are you going to try to find something better?"

"You bet - in fact, I think I'm going to drive around town Saturday and see what I can find," Katie replied in the same conspiratorial tone.

"Well, if you find anything interesting, keep me in the loop."

"Oh, but since you *like* Old Sourpuss *so* much, I just *assumed...* " Katie remarked sweetly.

"I do not," Derrik said defensively. He was no great fan of the QuickBurger either, although he was not as vehement as Katie. In Derrik's mind, a job was a job was a job, it was just for the money. It really didn't matter where or what the job was as long as it didn't get in the way of his *real* life.

No doubt there were better jobs out there, and he was always keeping his eyes and ears open, but Derrik never seemed to find time to actively look for something better. If the time ever arrived to get a new job, Derrik knew he could find one. The job market was great, and all of his friends who wanted to work were working.

Maybe Katie would find something fun and get him hired, too, Derrik reflected absently.

There are lots of jobs available - and every applicant knows it.

Becky: Not Looking

Earlier, when Katie was on her way to QuickBurger, she had parted company with her best friend, Becky Anderson, at the corner bus stop. Becky lived on the north side of town and would catch the next bus to her job as a salesclerk at Remington's, a women's clothing shop in the Northside Mall.

Unlike Katie, as far as Becky was concerned, her job was just fine. It put her in a mall and her co-workers and manager were pleasant enough. For someone her age, she felt like they gave her a great deal of responsibility.

Besides, to her, the job was hardly work at all. Becky's friendly, outgoing personality and positive attitude made her a natural at sales, and what could be better than using her eye for fashion to help less confident shoppers?

The managers at Remington's were pleased with Becky as well. Great service came naturally to her, and many customers insisted on having the fashionable young salesclerk assist them.

In Becky's mind, this job was ideal because it left most of her weekend evenings free, and the schedule was very flexible. This worked great because Becky wanted as much time as possible for important extracurricular activities - like dating.

Great employees are out there and they usually work for great companies. Traditional recruiting methods will never reach them.

Here's an overview of three of the different types of potential applicants Scott might want to pursue:

	Active Seeker	**Passive Seeker**	**Not Looking**[1]
Follows the job market:	Actively	Observing	Only a passing interest
Gathers information by:	Following employment ads, asking others, Internet, etc.	Listening to people	Only by happenstance
Receptivity:	Very open to discussion	Open to discussion	Willing to listen
Currently employed:	Maybe	Maybe	Highly likely
Time available for job hunting:	Will invest some time	Won't invest much time	Won't invest any time

In order to take a marketing approach to recruiting, you need to think about all potential recruits. Then tailor your message to appeal specifically to these people and put it where they're most likely to see it.

---

[1] "Not Looking" is still a job-seeking category - even if the prospective employee doesn't realize it. Nearly everyone is willing to at least *hear* about a new opportunity - and willing to be convinced another job may offer something they want.

CHAPTER 4 HIGHLIGHTS

Hourly employees are unlikely to tolerate a disagreeable situation for long.

There are lots of jobs available - and every applicant knows it.

Great employees are out there and they usually work for great companies. Traditional recruiting methods will never reach them.

CHAPTER 5:
Magnetic Company Basics

After his conversation with Tom, Scott realized why his previous tactics had fallen flat and convinced himself a marketing approach would be the key to successful recruiting. Perhaps in the old days a few signs and a classified ad would attract quality people, but in this market, a more sophisticated strategy was necessary. Everyone was after the best people and Scott knew Taylor's would have to become a magnetic company in order to attract them.

Then Scott recalled something else Tom had mentioned at dinner.

> *Create an environment that attracts*
> *the best employees naturally;*
> *don't rely on*
> *gimmicks and advertisements.*

"How can I do that?" wondered Scott. "In the minds of my ideal candidates, I must be first-choice as an employer. I have to attract them like - well, like a magnet, and draw them away from other service businesses if they're already working.

"I've heard from everyone that good employees want a fun, energetic atmosphere.

And they want to be with a company that looks like a winner."

Scott decided to visit his friend Sarah Costani, regional marketing manager for Taylor's. She was less than a 30-minute drive away, in the regional office.

"Hi, Scott," she said cheerfully when he appeared in her doorway. "I don't see your friendly face very often. What's up?"

"The usual," Scott replied, helping himself to one of the foil-wrapped chocolates in the candy dish on the corner of her desk. "John is under a lot of pressure from Donna to staff up, reduce turnover costs, and bring up customer-satisfaction scores. And John, in turn, is pressuring me to get more and better people hired - fast."

"So what are you doing here - hiding out?"

"Good idea, but no. I wanted to ask your advice. You see, I've recently decided I need to take more of a marketing approach to recruiting. To go after and attract employees the way you do customers."

"That makes sense. So how can I help?"

"I was wondering what your most effective strategies are for attracting customers," Scott replied. "Maybe I can borrow an idea or two. What works best for you?"

Sarah gazed out the window and thought for a moment. "Well, right now we're focusing on increasing the frequency and spending patterns of our current customers. We began the Frequent Buyers Club campaign with direct mail and in-store advertisements. We've taken a page from the airlines' book by letting customers earn free stuff and special discounts. With everything, we're emphasizing everyday low prices.

"Our latest strategy has been these grocery bag inserts," she said as she pulled out a rectangular card. "The baggers tuck these in the grocery bags. They include promotional offers for some of our most popular items. I know I'm reaching people who already visit and like Taylor's, and I'm encouraging them to return more often. I've had a terrific response."

Scott took one of the inserts. "I could definitely use this," he said enthusiastically. "Do you mind if I print up a recruiting message that would go in the bags with your marketing piece?"

"Not at all. I can't imagine that would hurt a bit. Glad to help."

Scott's next stop was Speedy Print. Ben Jordan, the owner, knew all of the Taylor's managers, and welcomed Scott warmly.

"What can I do for you today?" Ben asked.

"Two things, Ben. First, I need to get some new posters printed up." Scott produced one of the tired, old, red and white 'Help Wanted' signs that had hung in front of the store.

"I'd like to get new, laminated signs made up on high-quality paper with our logo and these new messages."

Ben flipped through Scott's handwritten notes of the revised recruiting messages: "Looking for Smiling Faces!" - "Come Join Our Team!" - "Be Pre-Approved for Our Next Employment Opportunity."

"How did you come up with these?" Ben asked.

"I borrowed some ideas from our Marketing Department," said Scott. "Aren't these a whole lot more upbeat and exciting than 'Now Hiring'? I really like that they don't scream 'short-staffed' or 'desperate' to potential employees or to the store's customers."

"It's a big improvement," Ben agreed.

Think of positive, creative ways to replace "Now Hiring" and "Help Wanted" signs.

"And while you print up these new signs," Scott continued, "I'll use the computer to design some grocery bag inserts."

In a few minutes, he had an attractive design telling shoppers Taylor's was "Offering Exciting Opportunities!" It included some of the key benefits of working for the supermarket and the Human Resource Department's phone number and e-mail address.

When the printing was complete, Scott took his new inserts and signs triumphantly back to Taylor's. He wasted no time in posting the new messages and telling all the baggers and cashiers about including the inserts with every customer's purchase.

Scott returned to work the next day, eagerly awaiting the deluge of applications he was hoping for. But not much happened. Over the next few days, applications did come in, but at basically at the same slow pace. There may have been some increase in volume, but if so, it was marginal. Several people did specifically mention the insert cards. All in all, not much happened and he was more than a little disappointed.

On Friday night, Scott, Tom, and their wives, Janet and Adrienne, got together for dinner. As they were finishing dessert, the women became engrossed in their own conversation, and Tom and Scott took the opportunity to pick up where they'd left off.

"How's your recruiting going, Scott?" asked Tom. "Have you put any marketing principles into action?"

"Well, to tell you the truth, they haven't done much for me. Maybe I just need to give it more time. But I don't *have* time."

"What happened?"

"Well, I spoke to our marketing manager, and asked her for ideas. She found grocery bag inserts are effective, so I tried that. And I hung new signs, too, with better messages. I suppose we've had more applicants, but not many more, and I wouldn't say the caliber of people applying is much better."

Tom thought for a moment and said, "It's great you thought to dovetail your recruiting messages with the marketing ones. The key is to have one communications strategy that supports both hiring and sales."

Leverage your marketing and recruiting efforts off of one another.

"I think the problem is that you've launched directly into tactics, without any overall strategic thought. Inserts are a good idea, plus, of course, you needed better signs. But that's only the beginning. There's so much more - you need a recruiting strategy and *system*, not just improved tactics."

"What do you mean, a system? I have signs, new inserts, and that classified ad is still running…"

"No, those are all tactics. Execution. You need a strategy. Let me explain.

"What you need to do, Scott, is design a recruiting system that's perfectly suited to Taylor's and its needs. In order to recruit effectively, you must know specifically what you're trying to achieve, and what the steps are. You can't just execute a step here, and a step there - and hope it turns out to be a tango.

"Let's look at it another way. Suppose you were the coach for a professional football team and your goal is to play in the Super Bowl. Obviously, you and your team are going to need a lot of practice, right?"

"Yes, of course."

"However, would your *very first step* be to just run everyone out on the field and start practicing?"

"Of course not," answered Scott. "Before the season even began, I'd make sure I made the most strategic trades and assembled the best team possible."

"Exactly. You would get your assistant coaches together, plan the workouts and practices, and figure out the equipment you'd need. You'd plan your practices to train your players without wearing them out or getting them injured, and the whole time you'd be consulting with the team owner, and physical therapist, and general manager, and a host of other people."

"What I'm getting at, Scott, is success - in anything - does not happen by accident. You're going to have to plan and execute a system. Right now, you've run out to the field to practice without doing any of the up-front work."

A company does not attract the best by accident.

"Now here's where you start," Tom said. "You have a system for accounting, right?" Scott nodded. "Someone at Taylor's could no doubt explain that system to me. What its overall purpose is, who runs the system, what its expected to produce, and what specific steps are taken in order to have useful records and reports. And you have an inventory control system, and a security system, and a billing system because they all make your jobs that much easier and make you more productive. That's why you need a recruiting system."

"That makes a lot of sense," admitted Scott.

Tom finished the last bite of his pecan pie and continued, "So that's your first step. You need to design a system. A process. A plan which will be in place and relevant to all of your future hiring.

If you're serious about recruiting great people, you have to get serious about your process.

"Second, you can't look at this hiring crisis as a one-time problem that can be solved with a one shot deal. All companies, even the very best, have turnover. It's the nature of the beast. People move away, go off to college, change their schedules, and change their lives.

"And you're going to want to promote your best people, which will create more jobs to fill. Recruiting is a never-ending process, and you should always have people waiting in the wings so you're never short-handed. Turnover is inevitable and your job is to get ahead of it, predict it, and manage it. You want to get things to where you have a pool of applicants to draw on whenever you need someone.

"But before you do anything, I want to warn you about the *very* worst thing you can do - and that's to make bad hiring decisions. You've got to stay committed to high hiring standards whether you have a system or not.

"It's going to take a while to get a firm grip on exactly what sort of employees you're looking for and you're still going to be desperate for new blood. Then some inferior candidate will walk in the door and you'll be tempted to hire that person as a short-term fix."

"I'm beginning to realize that, Tom," Scott replied. "I was just reading an article that said the number one reason good people leave is because of supervisors or co-workers with bad attitudes or lousy work habits."

"Just keep telling yourself, Scott, that there's nothing as expensive as a bad hire. You've got to stick to your plan, no matter how short-handed you get.

"Think of the turkeys you've hired in the past - oh, don't worry, we've all done it. They're far more expensive than they seem. Think about it. You've wasted all that time, energy, and money to recruit, screen, interview, and train them.

"And then you have to go through it all over again. It's aggravating and it puts a big dent in productivity. And what about the effects on the rest of your staff? Having a bad egg around sets a miserable example and brings everyone down. Then there's the time spent training both the bad hire and that person's replacement. On top of all this, you may lose customers due to your bad hire's attitude or your replacement's inexperience.

"I know it's tempting, when you're short-staffed and everyone is screaming for help, but if there's one thing I want you to keep in mind, it's this:

Never hire someone you wouldn't hire if you weren't desperate.

"For every person you think you might hire, ask yourself, 'How would I feel if this person went to work for the competition?' It's a great barometer to keep you from random acts of desperation hiring.

Tom continued, "Now, imagine the positive side. Think for a minute about your *best* hires - and think of a world where that's the only kind of people you have working for you.

"The best people pay for themselves over and over, don't they? They know their jobs, take pride in doing them well, and are always coming up with ideas for doing things better. They like to learn, and conversely can train the new people. In fact, they can usually train better than you can because they know the job better.

"They're good for morale - because they're easy to work with, carry their share of the load, and serve as an example to the others.

"And think about their effect on customers. Customers like to interact with people who are competent, knowledgeable, and efficient. It saves them time, money, and frustration.

"In this world, everyone on staff has good judgment and the ability to help customers with unexpected or unusual situations. Since this level of service is so rare, a customer will be exceptionally loyal to the organization that provides it.

"As you know, this is just the tip of the iceberg. But the point is:

Great employees are invaluable.
The time and money it takes to find them
generate a huge return-on-investment.

"So where do I go from here, Tom?" asked Scott somewhat overwhelmed, but grateful for all the new insight.

"Tell you what. I'm teaching my class next Tuesday morning. Why don't we get together for lunch, and I'll help you get started? Come by my office at the school around 11:30."

"That would be great," Scott replied in appreciation. "Just for the record, what is my next step?"

"Now that we've laid some groundwork so to speak, what we'll do next is identify the potential applicants you'll target. You know you can't hit a target if you don't know what it looks like - so I'll help you define exactly what it is you're looking for."

That Monday morning, back in his office, Scott summarized in writing the points he'd learned from Tom on Friday night.

CHAPTER 5 HIGHLIGHTS

*Create an environment
that attracts the best employees naturally; don't
rely on gimmicks and advertisements.*

*Think of positive, creative ways to replace "Now
Hiring" and "Help Wanted" signs.*

*Leverage your marketing and
recruiting efforts off of each other.*

*A company does not attract the best
by accident.*

*If you're serious about recruiting great people,
you have to be serious about your process.*

*Never hire someone you wouldn't hire if you
weren't desperate.*

*Great employees are immensely valuable. The
time and money it takes to find them generate a
huge return-on-investment.*

The Costs of a Bad Hire	The Value of a Good Hire
Inefficiencies due to the position being vacant.	Saves training time; learns quickly, trains others.
Costs of disappointing, even alienating, customers.	Satisfies or even delights customers who become loyal shoppers and word-of-mouth advertisers.
Time spent finding, screening, and training replacements.	The morale boost of working with someone pleasant, capable, and hard working.
Bad morale caused by a difficult personality, bad attitude, or a person who is a slacker.	A contagious, positive attitude and a good example.
Direct advertising and hiring costs, such as a newspaper classified ads, background checks, drug tests, etc.	The good judgment necessary to know when to step outside of a defined role or to bend the rules for a customer.
The stress of having to fire someone.	Takes the initiative.
The aggravation of having to start over.	Suggests innovations and improvements.
Inefficiencies of co-workers closely associated with new employees and inefficiencies of departing employees.	Easy to manage – and saves *your* time and co-workers' time.

CHAPTER 6:
The Job Analysis

To prepare for his lunch with Tom, Scott gave some thought to the systematic marketing concept they'd discussed. By this time he realized his new tactics - different hiring signs, insert cards, and so on - were fine, but what was needed was to orchestrate them with other new strategies into a cohesive system.

Scott left Taylor's at 11:00 and drove to Tom's office on campus. As soon as they were seated over their sandwiches in the cafeteria, Tom began to outline the first steps in Scott's recruiting strategy.

"First of all, Scott, it's essential to know what you're looking for," Tom pointed out. "The main reason we don't hire the best people, and in fact sometimes hire the worst, is because we don't know what a good employee looks like.

"Here's an analogy you'll appreciate, Scott - grocery shopping."

"What's the connection?" asked Scott.

"Well, what's the number one thing you need when you go grocery shopping?"

"Money," answered Scott promptly.

"Other than that."

Scott looked blank. "Well, I don't know," he faltered. "I suppose you need a car or something...?"

"What you need is a list. Otherwise, what happens? We've all done it. First, you don't get everything you need. Second, you do get things you really *don't* need. Then, you spend more time and money than you intended, and, finally, what happens? You have to go back to the store to get what you really needed in the first place.

"This is exactly what happens when you try to shop for an employee without knowing what you need. Most grocery shoppers eventually learn to make a list first - but somehow, a lot of recruiting managers never do."

> *Looking for an employee without knowing what you need is like grocery shopping without a list.*

"Well, I just kind of assumed I know since I've been at the store so long," remarked Scott.

"That's another common misconception," said Tom. "Jobs and the best kinds of people to fill them change all the time. It's better to pretend you don't know anything and then figure out what you need *before* you start getting people. Then you won't get more or less than you need or waste time and money on unqualified applicants. What you need to do next is list the key attributes necessary for your ideal candidate."

If you know exactly what you're looking for, you're much more likely to find it.

"All right. So I need a shopping list for my ideal candidates, is what you're telling me. Is this the same thing as a job description?" Scott asked.

"Good question. A job description gets you in the ballpark, but what I'd rather see you do is a job analysis. The job descriptions most employers use only cover the essential functions of the job - the specific things the person needs to be able to do. A job analysis, on the other hand, goes into more detail. It's paints a better picture of reality."

"How do I write a job analysis?" Scott queried in the midst of his note taking.

"First, consider the reason the job exists. Why is it essential to Taylor's? What are you trying to accomplish?

"Next, you'll want to define the objectives of the job and the employee's responsibilities. Here - I'll give you a list of questions to ask yourself:

1. What must the jobholder do well to earn a raise or bonus?

2. Why would you reprimand or fire someone holding this job?

3. What did the last jobholder do well and not so well?

4. What would you like to see done differently?

5. What has kept jobholders from being successful in the past?

6. What do you want to make sure nobody in this job ever does again?

"Ask yourself these questions, Scott, and you'll be amazed at how it changes what you look for in a candidate."

"You know," Scott reflected, "I'm absolutely certain I couldn't answer all of those for a couple of our open positions. I know about the jobs I used to hold, but we have several new positions I'm just not that familiar with."

"Well, there's part of your problem - and you probably have some outdated assumptions about the jobs you do know. You'll need to spend some time asking employees and managers these questions. Spend some time just observing too. You'll be far more qualified to hire employees when you know, exactly, what they're supposed to do."

Tom continued, "Go into as much detail as you possibly can. Does the job change under any circumstances? What differences exist between the morning shift and the evening shift, for example?"

Scott remarked, "Well, this certainly does give me a lot of work to do. And you're saying to do this job analysis for every position I have?"

"Every one where it matters what sort of employee holds it."

"That's all of them," sighed Scott.

"Here are a few other pointers to keep in mind," continued Tom. "Make sure you stay focused on essentials when you sit down to write them. I've discovered it's easy to get carried away and turn a job analysis into an unrealistic wish list.

"But be creative at the same time. Think about different ways the potential employee could carry out his or her duties. There may be other ways to get the job done you haven't considered.

"And remember, the analysis needs to change and adapt with time. Your company is always changing, and so are the roles of the people in it. Take into account new or different responsibilities, technological innovations, management changes, things like that.

A job description is like a snapshot; a job analysis is like a motion picture.

"When you're finished, what you'll have for each position is a detailed profile of the qualities and abilities necessary to be successful on the job. And you'll find it absolutely revolutionizes the way you hire."

"Well," Scott responded, "what you're saying sounds like common sense, but the reality is that this has never occurred to me, nor has anyone else ever suggested it."

"I know," answered Tom. "It really is a different hiring model. But let me give you a few more pointers since we're on a roll. Most of the time this won't be true for you at Taylor's, but sometimes there's a possibility you don't actually need to go out and hire.

"Normally you hire to fill a position someone has vacated or because growth requires more employees. But, as you fill out a job analysis, be open to the possibility the job could be eliminated."

"How's that?" asked Scott.

"Think about alternatives to hiring. Could you possibly assign part or all of it to existing employees or use temporary workers, or job-sharing? And don't overlook the good people already on staff. You don't always have to go outside to fill a position - especially if it would mean a promotion for someone. Nothing's better for employee morale and motivation than seeing co-workers promoted.

"Or possibly technology - like those electronic, self-service check-out counters they're testing - could eliminate the need for a position altogether. Word processing replaced a lot of typists and secretaries. Accounting software has reduced the need for accountants; the scanners at Taylor's mean cashiers no longer need to know prices; self-service gas and pay-at-the-pump reduced the number of service station attendants. And, of course, lots of companies use an automated, voice mail system instead of hiring people to answer the telephone. Many of the things that have to be done to keep a business going can be outsourced to vendors too."

Automation and outsourcing may be cost-efficient and may also eliminate the need for a position.

"Alternatively, you might be able to change the process," Tom continued.

"What do you mean by that?" said Scott with a puzzled look.

"Well, many fast-food restaurants, for example, now have self-serve beverage bars which eliminate the need for a person to stand behind the counter to fill drink orders.

"Another example is convenience stores. Many of them have abandoned the sale of lottery tickets because the extra effort required to staff, monitor, and prevent fraud didn't justify the revenue. These are just examples, and obviously aren't always relevant. The point is, think it through. Make sure you need to hire."

Hiring is not always the answer.

CHAPTER 6 HIGHLIGHTS

Looking for an employee without knowing what you need is like grocery shopping without a list.

If you know exactly what you're looking for, you're much more likely to find it.

A job description is like a snapshot; a job analysis is like a motion picture.

There may be alternatives to hiring a new, permanent, full-time worker.

Automation and outsourcing may be cost-efficient and may also eliminate the need for a position.

Hiring is not always the answer.

CHAPTER 7:
How to Write a Job Analysis

Scott spent the next few days doing the needed research so he could write a job analysis for each of his open positions. As expected, it took a lot of time and thought, but the payoff was that he found the process to be a real revelation.

He started by simply walking around the store. He spent time observing employees in action and made notes about their responsibilities and roles. The next day, he began interviewing all of the stores' staff and management to get more information on what each position required.

Scott also surveyed former employees by phone. What he learned made him resolve to start conducting exit interviews whenever anyone gave notice.

"From now on," thought Scott, "when a good employee decides to move on, I'll find out why and see if it's possible to turn the situation around. I'll also ask for more information about the nature and responsibilities of the job so I can hire an even better fit the next time."

Scott discovered there was a lot to be learned from poor performers as well. Many told him they didn't understand everything they would be expected to do when they accepted the offer. Scott reviewed the decision-making process that led to each of these less-than-desirable hires and concluded that he could save everyone a great deal of frustration by spelling out, in detail, up front, all of the job's responsibilities.

> *Exit interviews are excellent sources of information, but most companies don't conduct them.*

After reviewing all the data he'd collected, Scott was ready to call Tom to arrange another get-together.

"What's next?" he asked his friend on the telephone. "You said to call when I finished the job analysis forms. I did them and you were right. I've learned a lot about our employees and their jobs."

Tom said he'd be happy to get together again and agreed to meet Scott, same time, same place, the following Tuesday.

"It's overwhelming, isn't it?" Tom asked while looking through Scott's pages of notes. "It would be easy to run off in a hundred different directions. What we have to do is focus on the essentials.

"So, today let's discuss attitude. It's a crucial element of your job analyses because it further defines exactly who and what you're looking for.

"As you've probably realized, the jobs you're hiring for aren't in the rocket science category. Most people, with reasonable training and resources, could do these jobs. Right?"

"Yes, definitely."

"Then why do so many people fail? Why do you have so much trouble filling the positions with quality employees?"

"I wish I knew," answered Scott.

"I'll tell you what makes the difference," Tom replied. "It's attitude. You need people who enjoy working, who care about the quality of their work, who are dependable, and easy to get along with. These are the team players who like helping other people - namely your customers and their co-workers."

> *You can't train someone to*
> *smile or be dependable.*

"True" Scott agreed, "but I've recognized this all along. I think everyone who hires knows how important attitude is."

"Yes and no," Tom replied. "Managers do try to hire reliable, friendly people because we've all been through the headaches of dealing with bad attitudes.

"There are, however, two problems. First, managers underestimate how crucial attitude is, and sometimes hire only for skills or experience. What's needed is a better understanding of the relative importance of attitudes and skills.

"Second, managers usually have no basis for judging attitude other than the vague impressions they gather during interviews. Managers need a better way to find out what attitudes an applicant will bring to the job. Remember, if you don't know *exactly* what you're looking for, you can't find it - unless you're unusually lucky."

"So how can I stack the odds more in my favor?" asked Scott.

"You begin, as you have, with the job analysis. Once you understand what the key responsibilities are for each position, and what you're looking for, then you use the CAPS model."

"The what?" asked Scott.

"In the CAPS model, 'C' stands for capacities, 'A' for attitudes, 'P' is for personality, and 'S' is for skills," replied Tom, as if it were perfectly obvious.

"Well, now I know why you're one of the best teachers here," Scott observed. "I should have known you'd come up with an acronym."

"The thinking behind my acronym is that there are some basics a person simply must have in order to be considered for the position. First and foremost are physical and mental capacities required to do the job. The nicest person in the world with the best attitude does me no good if she can't physically or mentally do the work.

"After capacities, come attitudes. As I said a minute ago, you simply can't pay too much attention to this.

"You know how some people *can* do the job - but just *won't*? The complainers, the no-shows, the lazy ones?"

Scott nodded.

"That's what attitude covers. In your particular case, I would expand it so you cover not just dependability - which, of course, most every job requires - but also customer service, honesty, and the willingness to go outside of the job description in order to tackle the task at hand."

Scott nodded again and said, "No question about it, attitude is critical to success.

The number-one reason to hire or fire an hourly employee is attitude.

"Next comes personality. In the kinds of jobs we're talking about, it's nowhere near as important as attitude and capacities, but it does play a role. For instance, a guy with the basic capacities and a terrific attitude, but is too shy to talk to customers isn't going to make a great cashier, but he could be just right as a stocker. Certain personality traits are preferable for certain jobs.

"Understand, Scott, personality is *not* the same thing as attitude - although sometimes the lines are blurred. Personality encompasses characteristics such as extroversion, competitiveness, and sociability.

"The key to remember about personality is that it can be managed by attitude. People usually choose their responses to situations and that manifests itself as personality. So many managers hire on the basis of whether or not they "like" someone, without understanding how that person's personality may change when exposed to stress, difficulty, or fatigue."

"I'm not sure I'm following," Scott said.

"When managers think they're looking for attitude, it's usually personality traits they're assessing. But personality traits are *not* attitudes. Imagine a person who is cheerful, friendly, and talkative, but is blatantly dishonest and irresponsible.

"And think of another who is quiet and shy but incredibly intelligent, easygoing, and hard-working. While you would not want the first person to hold any position at Taylor's, regardless of how likable he might be, the second person would probably make an excellent employee.

"Thinking they're looking for attitudes, managers will often hire the first and not the second. They never get around to finding out about responsibility and honesty until it's too late.

"Again, the point is there are no hard and fast rules when it comes to personality. You just need to determine if any particular personality traits are necessary for each job."

"This makes a ton of sense," Scott observed. "I can see how this will help me interview - I did try to hire for attitude before, but now that you've explained it, I think I did just look for personality 'click' - someone I liked.

Look for the person who is best for the job not the person you like best.

Not being one to leave any bases uncovered, Tom continued, "Personality fit can be important in smaller organizations where an individual with a radically different style might not fit in. Communications breakdowns and a feeling of not belonging can often cause an employment disaster. So, keep personality traits in mind, but don't mistake them for attitude.

"Next, and last, in the CAPS model are skills - the specific abilities you can't or won't train for. This means you need to hire people with training or experience. At Taylor's, you probably don't have too many skill requirements - except for the butcher or the person at the seafood counter, or, possibly, in your bookkeeping office.

"Do you require prospective cashiers to have prior experience?"

"No," Scott replied, "we have a good training program."

"Well," said Tom, "some grocers do require experience. But in actuality, if you have someone who's bright and eager-to-learn, I'd bet it doesn't take long to learn the register."

"Right, again," said Scott.

"I figured as much, but the important point I want to make is that for most customer service, entry-level people, you can almost always train for the skills you need, provided you begin with core capacities and have someone with the right attitudes."

Hire for attitude, train for skills.

"The last step in this process is that at the same time you make it easy to apply, you make your jobs harder to get. You ask specific questions of the applicants and their references dealing with the CAPS requirements that are essential. Depending on the job, you may want to give math and physical ability or intellectual capacity tests. Just because someone says they can do something, doesn't mean it's so. If it's in writing - in your job analysis - not only can you ask applicants if they can perform the task, you can ask them to demonstrate their proficiency. If a particular skill is a requirement, always test for it.

"Just consult your lawyer first. Some things are a little tricky - especially physical capacity tests - and you want to stay in compliance with the Americans with Disabilities Act as well.

"Give paper-and-pencil or computerized attitude tests. This is the best possible way to use the applicant's time instead of yours to get all kinds of useful information about things like honesty and dependability. It's really a way to get applicants to interview themselves for you. Pre-employment testing is far and away the most reliable predictor of success on the job. The only other thing you can do that even comes close to predicting success as well is a temporary job assignment. Even reference checks are only half as reliable. To many people's surprise, past experience, the interview, and academic achievement are three of the least reliable predictors of how a person will do. And the biggest myth of all is that age has anything to do with job performance.

"Another important test is for drugs. If most of your competitors for employees are testing for drugs and you're not, where do you think the drug users will apply? At the very least put 'Ours is a drug-free workplace' in your ads and on a sign in the hiring office. Drug testing need not slow up the process either. You can extend a conditional job offer contingent on the results of this test.

"Essentially, there are only two ways to handle the hiring process. You can hire tough or hire easy. Most employers take the hire easy approach - especially when it comes to hourly employees.

"Hire easy means applicants merely need to pass the *breath test*[1] in order to start work. If they can fog a mirror with their breath, they're hired. When an employer puts such little value on the job, that's exactly the value and effort employees will put into that job. Most likely, they'll be poor performers and problem employees who require constant attention. Their employers will need to have exceptional management skills - and stamina. The less you expect in the hiring process and the easier the job is to get, the more time and money you're going to spend trying to get the people you hire to do what you need them to.

"The reverse is also true. The harder the job is to get, the better the quality of the people you attract and the easier and less time-consuming the manager's job becomes. And the kicker is that when you make your jobs hard to get, it makes the outstanding people want to work for you even more. The best and brightest naturally figure that if the job is hard to get, then the employer is serious about doing things right, and the organization must be an extraordinarily good one to work for. Also, the people who think 'it's only a job' will deselect themselves and not go through your process or simply won't do well."[2]

Make the job easy to apply for and hard to get.

As he drove back to his office after the meeting, Scott mulled over the implications of

---

[2] To learn how to create a hiring system, see *Hire Tough, Manage Easy - How to Find & Hire the Best Hourly Employees*. (For more information, visit www.hiretough.com.)

the CAPS model and what he could do to start creating a hire tough system. He couldn't wait to use all he'd learned about recognizing and hiring quality employees. And he was anxious to take a second pass at those job analysis forms.

In the past, Scott had reviewed employment applications for experience or skills first, and then looked for that personality click in the interview. He'd given no real thought to basic capacities and had been confusing attitudes with personality traits.

He realized he'd probably screened out lots of candidates who might have been perfect with a little training. And by failing to understand what attitude really is, Scott had saddled Taylor's with several people who were cheerful and outgoing enough in their interviews, but had turned out to be undependable goof-offs on the job.

Scott's next task was to fill out the CAPS requirements for each of his open positions. Getting the detailed lists of the necessary core capacities, attitudes, personality traits, and skills didn't take long because he'd done such a good job on his research work.

If you don't know what - or whom - you're looking for, you'll never find it.

Right after he finished, Scott remembered Tom's caution about unrealistic wish lists. After all, a bilingual, experienced cashier who could work completely flexible hours might be hard to find.

Did he really *need* all that? Experience was certainly a plus, but an intelligent, customer service-oriented person could be easily trained. And most of the shifts could be scheduled. What he really needed was a bilingual person with the requisite physical and mental capacities, a good attitude, and willingness to come in and cover during staff shortages from time to time.

Know the difference between what you need to have and what would be nice to have.

Scott then reviewed all his work and crossed out the unnecessary requirements. When he'd finished, he felt the final job analysis forms spelled out what it would take to be a successful employee in every position he was currently hiring for.

Let's take a look at one...

CAPS JOB ANALYSIS
POSITION: CASHIER

Capacities	Attitudes	Personality	Skills
Reliable transportation to and from work. Physical ability to be on feet all day and to lift heavy grocery items. Bending, stooping, reaching. Good eyesight and hearing. Physical dexterity to handle cash, coins, credit cards, and coupons. Ability to learn systems and procedures.	Willingness to work some extra shifts at times. Honesty. Dependability. Initiative to work around problems. Customer service-orientation (likes working with people). Willingness to go outside of job description.	Outgoing. High energy level. Good attention to detail. Able to follow through. Wants to be part of a team.	Bilingual (English/Spanish) Basic math Read, write, and communicate at 9th grade level

CHAPTER 7 HIGHLIGHTS

*Exit interviews and surveys of former employees
are excellent sources of information.*

*Because you can't train someone
to smile or be dependable,
the right attitudes are essential.*

*The number-one reason
to hire or fire an hourly employee is attitude.*

*Look for the person who is best for the job - not
the person you like best.*

Hire for attitudes, train for skills.

Make the job easy to apply for, and hard to get.

*If you don't know what - or whom -
you're looking for, you'll never find it.*

*Know the difference between what you need to
have and what would be nice to have.*

CHAPTER 8:
The Jobseeker's Experience

Let's check in again with our potential recruits...

It was a warm and sunny Saturday. As Katie surveyed her closet for something she felt like wearing, she bravely resisted a temptation to just hang out in her room with her favorite music and magazines, and resolutely pushed all thoughts of shopping - in spite of the spring sales going on - out of her mind.

"Today is the day I find a new job," she told herself. "I've put it off too long. I can't wait to see the look on Becky's face when I tell her my days at QuickBurger are over."

Spurred on by this cheering thought, Katie convinced her mother to loan her the car for the day, and set off.

Downtown seemed the most logical place to begin. It was only a five-minute drive from Katie's house, and so many Lincoln High students went there after school every day that transportation to a job nearby would be a breeze.

In her mind, Katie was already liberated from QuickBurger. She was eager to have a predictable schedule, lose the heat and grease, and, most of all, lose Old Sourpuss.

She imagined her next job full of interesting people, rapid promotion, and an appreciative manager at a place her friends would think was cool.

Once downtown, Katie parked and walked around, looking for possibilities. She was immediately struck by the number of 'Help Wanted' signs she saw, one after another. "It's great so many stores are hiring," Katie reflected, "but this is overwhelming. How will I choose?"

It reminded her of the local paper's classified ads, which, at her mother's suggestion, she'd scanned through last night. There had been so many ads and so little information, it proved a useless exercise. She surfed the Web for a while too, but she wasn't about to fill out an on-line application when she didn't have a feel for what the place was really like. Were the employees having a good time? What was the dress code? She'd have to check things out herself.

It's essential to differentiate yourself, especially in challenging hiring markets.

"Well, I have to begin somewhere," Katie thought. She was standing in front of the Lindy Hop, a trendy clothing store for young women. Although Katie usually patronized the Northside Mall, the Lindy Hop was popular with lots of her classmates.

They would be extremely impressed to see her there. And she could get the employee discount. Katie pushed open the door and walked in.

Image is everything.
Potential recruits are attracted to you
based on image, not reality.

"Hi, can I help you?" said the chirpy young woman who bounded from behind the sales counter.

"Yes, could I have an application, please?"

"Oh." The salesclerk was visibly deflated. She returned to the counter and started rummaging through papers. Katie waited patiently when the clerk stopped to explain the details of the layaway policy to a browser. As she shifted from foot to foot, she examined the sale rack to pass the time.

Eventually the clerk finished her conversation and produced a faded photocopy of the store's employment application. "Over here," she called, as she dropped the form on the counter and turned her attention to an older woman who had just walked in.

"I'd forgotten what a hassle this is," Katie thought, as she began to fill it out. She was halfway through the personal information when she was interrupted.

"Sorry, but could you fill it out somewhere else?" the salesclerk asked. "I need this space for the customers."

Katie snatched up her belongings and stepped aside. "Oh, of course, I'm sorry." She looked around but didn't see anywhere else suitable.

"Where should I …?"

"You can fill it out at home and bring it back," the young woman suggested.

"All right," Katie agreed. "When I get to this reference section, can you tell me if they want job references only or can I use teachers?"

"I really don't know," answered the clerk sharply, laying down an armful of clothes on the counter, obviously losing her patience. "Why don't you call our manager in a few hours, things might be slower then, but I'm afraid right now we're *very busy.*"

Feeling like an unwitting interloper, Katie left as quickly as she could. Once outside, she threw the application in the first trashcan she passed.

"I can *definitely* do better than that. What an awful person. See if I *ever* go back there to shop!"

It's vital to educate your staff on the importance and etiquette of recruiting. A bad experience can lose you a potential employee or disenchant someone who might have become a customer.

Katie kept walking. A few blocks later, the European Café caught her eye. It was warm and cozy inside with exposed brick walls and a central firepit. Four waitresses were bustling about delivering desserts and coffee drinks to the customers seated at tables draped with fresh, white linen tablecloths.

Katie watched the scene for a few minutes and felt her hopes rise. "This looks great," she told herself. The waitresses wore hunter green aprons and white shirts and shorts - already better than the orange polyester and caps at QuickBurger.

And they seemed to be having fun. "Who wouldn't have fun?" Katie thought, eyeing the case of elaborate desserts. In light of her recent experience, she approached the counter a little apprehensively.

"I noticed your 'Help Wanted' sign," she began. "May I have an application?"

"Yes, of course." A clean sheet of heavy, cream colored paper, with a gold, embossed logo was produced. "Why don't you sit over there to fill this out," the hostess suggested, indicating a small table, "and I'll bring you a pen and something to drink, on us. What would you like?"

Katie was impressed. She filled out the form over a foamy iced mocha drink and sternly told herself she was going to have to exercise more often to compensate for all the yummy sweets on hand here. In her mind she already worked for the European Café, the rest was mere formality.

The hostess accepted Katie's application graciously. "Thank you very much. I'll give this to our manager. You should hear from us in a week or two and we can set up an interview for you then."

Surprised, Katie asked, "Isn't there any way to do this sooner?"

"I'm afraid not. Dan isn't even in until Tuesday - he handles our hiring. But I'll tell you what - I'll ask him to get to this as soon as possible. How's that?"

"Great," Katie said agreeably, although she was disappointed. By the time a decision was made, it could be weeks, and she'd hoped for something new today.

"Maybe I'm expecting too much," she thought. "Well, no harm in continuing to look. This can be my backup."

***Making a great impression may not be enough.
If your process is too slow,
you may lose applicants to faster competitors.***

Katie passed several more "Now Hiring" and "Help Wanted" signs. She walked past most of them without going in. She didn't know exactly what she was looking for, but at each business she imagined herself working there and a crowd of her classmates walking in. Many establishments failed this unofficial "Lincoln High Test."

The next stop was a popular casual-dining restaurant specializing in gourmet burgers. In Katie's mind, it had potential - young, energetic employees in attractive uniforms.

It was also part of a national chain, which, in her mother's opinion, would make the experience even more valuable. When she went to college in a few years, it might be easier to find a new part-time job if local employers recognized the chain's name, or, better yet, she might be able to transfer to one of their locations near the campus.

But Katie's hopes were to suffer yet another setback. She was astonished when she was handed *three* forms - one asking for a detailed life history, one for references, and even a mini-essay. There was no possibility of filling them out - she didn't have all the necessary information, the time, or inclination.

"I'll take them home," Katie decided. "Maybe during the week I can get around to them."

Make your jobs easy to apply for.

As she continued her downtown tour, Katie stopped in several more stores, restaurants, and offices. When deciding whether or not to complete an application, she relied on instinct and first impressions. Was the store nicely designed and clean? Did the employees look friendly? Did it look like fun? How was she treated? By the time she had to start back home, Katie had filled out seven applications.

"Well, I may not have anything yet," she reflected, "but I've planted quite a few seeds and I'm sure I'll have something in a few days. I'm glad I did this today."

As she passed Taylor's Grocery, a sign in the window caught Katie's eye. After a day of 'Help Wanted' messages, this looked appealing:

> **Come Grow With Us!**
> **Join Taylor's Team for**
> **Fun, Flexibility and**
> **Promotion Opportunities!**

Since this was exactly what she was looking for, Katie decided to turn in one more application. She still had plenty of time before her double date with Becky that night.

When she got inside she looked around and asked a bagger she knew from school where she should go. He pointed the way and as she made her way to the office in the back, Katie's decision to apply was reinforced. It was a clean, well-lit, busy store. It did look like fun - there were so many different things to do, it couldn't be boring.

At the office, Katie was warmly received, and there was counter space set aside for people to fill out applications. The man who greeted her was able to answer her questions, and Katie was able to finish the paperwork in less than 30 minutes.

When she turned it in, Ed Cantu, the young man behind the counter, took a moment to review the information and said, "This looks real good, Katie. Can we do an interview now?"

Katie was flattered and her estimation of Taylor's grew. She may have been only a QuickBurger employee, but clearly Taylor's recognized potential.

As a matter of fact, Ed's new marching orders were to verbally pre-screen promising applicants on the spot. It was one of Scott's many recent changes. During the hours applications were accepted, Ed and Janice Lebowitz, Scott's two assistants, now alternated as greeters because Scott had schooled them in the importance of providing great "customer service" to all applicants.

They now accepted the applications themselves and, if a person looked promising, asked the new set of pre-screening questions. If the applicant passed that test too, he or she would be given a pre-employment attitude exam on the PC set up just for that purpose. If the exam results indicated the person would be reliable, honest, and customer-service oriented, the applicant would be kicked upstairs to interview with Scott or, if he wasn't available, scheduled to meet with him as soon as possible.

When Scott was training Ed and Janice in these new procedures, Janice asked why they would do the attitude test before the interview. "Wouldn't we save money if we only test the people we think we want to hire?"

Scott explained that by testing for attitudes before the interview, he wouldn't waste any time interviewing people who may be risky new hires and that the test results would indicate the best kinds of interview questions to ask the applicant. "Besides," Scott said, "if I like how the interview goes and then the person doesn't pass the attitude evaluation, I've just shot myself in the foot."

As far as Ed was concerned, Katie had all the right answers to the pre-screen, she passed the attitude evaluation with flying colors, and met the capacity and skills criteria, so he paged Scott to set up her interview with him. Scott was free and told Ed to send her right up.

Then, while Katie was visiting with Scott, Ed phoned her references to verify the information she had provided. Luck was with Katie that day; Ed was able to reach every one of them.

After Scott had taken her through the structured interview he had recently written, he asked her to wait for a few minutes. After consulting with Ed, Scott returned to his office.

"Well, Ed and I both enjoyed meeting you, and we think you would be a great fit at Taylor's. We would like to offer you an entry-level position."

Katie was thrilled. The pay was competitive, even slightly better than QuickBurger, and the store had a training program she thought she would like. She smiled to herself when she remembered that a cute guy from homeroom, Michael Kelleher, worked at this Taylor's too.

"Who knows when - or if - these other places will call," Katie thought. "I should take advantage of this opportunity."

Katie accepted the job. She couldn't wait to tell Old Sourpuss and Becky the news.

CHAPTER 8 HIGHLIGHTS

It's essential to differentiate yourself,
especially in challenging hiring markets.

Image is everything.
Potential recruits are attracted by image,
not reality.

The initial experience is critical.
Frontline staff needs to understand
the importance and etiquette of recruiting.

Making a great impression may not be enough.
If your process is too slow,
you may lose applicants to faster competitors.

Make your jobs easy to apply for and
hard to get.

Lose the "Now Hiring" and
"Help Wanted" signs.

Use creative messages and signs
to differentiate yourself from your competition.

CHAPTER 9:
Attracting More Applicants

A week later, Scott and Tom were back at the Riverview Café, polishing off their fried chicken and mashed potatoes and contemplating the dessert offerings.

Their discussions over the past few weeks had proven beneficial to both. Scott had learned a lot from his friendly mentor, and felt ready to take on even more. Tom was enjoying this opportunity to put his hard-won experience into action. He'd spent years learning these recruiting techniques and enjoyed seeing them put into practice from the ground up. Scott's experiences were also a good source of anecdotes and case studies for his classes.

"So how's recruiting going these days, Scott?" Tom asked.

"I've seen some real improvement," replied Scott. "I feel more in control since I've committed to this plan and established high hiring standards. I think we're ready to really swing into action."

"I'm glad to hear that because I think you're ready for Phase Two."

"Phase Two?"

"That's right. Now that you've laid the foundation and worked out a strategy, it's time to start putting it all into action."

Plan your work and work your plan.

"Actually," Tom added, "you still have Phase Three left, too. Think of Phase Two as increasing the quantity of applicants and Phase Three as increasing the quality."

"This sounds exciting. Tell me more," said Scott.

"Let's recap first. Phase One was just laying the foundation. First you had to be committed and understand the importance of taking a marketing approach to recruiting.

"Then you analyzed exactly what you were looking for, in terms of the positions you were trying to fill, and the types of people who could fill them. Right?"

"Right," Scott nodded.

"Phase Two is where you become a *magnetic company*. Up until now we've just talked about that. Here's where you're going to make it happen. First you'll analyze your business from the perspective of potential applicants and then make every improvement you possibly can, until Taylor's is a first-rate organization from an employee's point of view."

"And Phase Three?" asked Scott.

"Phase Three is just reeling them in.

"Now that you've taken the first steps toward building an image that attracts recruits - it's time for you to learn how to pick the applicants who are *your* first choice. And I have lots of strategies for you to get the word out and the great employees in."

"I'm sold. What do I have to do to get rolling?" queried Scott.

"Begin with a thorough analysis."

"More analyzing?" asked Scott.

"Yes, but this time you want to look at Taylor's through the eyes of an employee and be realistic about the good, the bad, and the ugly. In order to get your arms around this, you need to get out there and *talk* with employees, past, present, and potential."

"What sort of questions should I ask?"

Tom rolled off a list: "What do I have to offer an hourly employee? What does a good employee want in the first place? How does my store look? How safe is it? What's special about working here? How are the other employees doing, and how's the morale?

"And for the employees you've lost: Why did they leave? Why didn't they succeed? What didn't they like? How could Taylor's improve? How could Taylor's win the good ones back?

"Don't forget to check out your competitors, too, Scott," added Tom. "They're a great source of ideas - good and bad. You'll see things you need to start doing, and things you should definitely avoid."

"And what's your reputation with customers? Don't forget, Scott, people like to be associated with winners. The most popular store in town will naturally have an easier time recruiting. You can improve employer-appeal *and* sales by addressing these issues.

"Always think of it in the context of competitive advantage. Get out there and see what's going on at the other grocery stores in town, and, more importantly, at all the other businesses that compete for the same kinds of employees. Get a sense of what it would be like to work for them. Remember the old adage, "Never mind what *you think* - ask a customer."

Scott nodded.

"Well, now it's time to say, never mind what *you* think - ask an employee. And then you begin to improve. Oh, I know you can't really give people everything they might wish for. People would like to be paid $20 an hour, but that isn't going to happen.

Know who you are and what you have to offer.

"But that isn't their number one concern anyway, and you don't differentiate yourself from the competition by paying ten cents an hour more."

Scott took all this down on his trusty notepad, and resolved to begin Phase Two the next day.

The next morning, to keep himself focused, he pinned a large sign to his wall:

Never mind what you think - ask an employee.

Which is exactly what Scott did. He talked with the department managers. He talked with the checkers, baggers, deli staff, butcher, bakers, and the cleaning crew. Scott was a man on a mission.

At first, the employees were suspicious, hesitant to share their thoughts. But once they were convinced he was really interested, a floodgate opened.

Scott found notes on his desk, in his in-box, and one was even mailed to his home. Employees approached him to talk about what they liked, what they didn't like, and what their friends thought.

And he *really listened*.

> ***You'll be amazed at what you learn
> and begin to achieve effortlessly
> by simply listening to your employees.***

Scott didn't limit his research to only Taylor's employees. He made it a point to visit other companies and talk to their people. He even interviewed five neighborhood teenagers.

Over the next week, Scott's grasp of the needs and desires of the staff grew. Just as Tom had predicted, he noticed he was beginning to "think like an employee." It was a definite shift in his point of view, but somehow a liberating one.

Even before Scott began to make some needed changes, he noticed something interesting happening. Although not much time had elapsed, turnover had begun to trend down for the first time in many months.

"I wonder - is it possible - that just listening to what's on people's minds, has resulted in some intangible morale boost?" To be on the safe side, Scott decided to assume it had, and resolved to keep in touch with the "floor" from now on.

As the issues came into clear focus, Scott turned his attention to writing a proposed plan of action to remedy those situations where the need was most critical.

As manager of Human Resources, Scott was able and authorized to implement some of the needed changes on his own. Others required executive support and resources, as well as acceptance by all the mid-level managers.

Scott knew it would be impossible to implement change without everyone else on the management team buying-in - especially his store manager.

The only way to revolutionize recruiting and hiring is to get management buy-in.

At the next manager meeting, Scott presented what he'd learned and done so far and said, "If we're going to enjoy the success we all want, it will be generated by the folks on the frontline. So they've got to be the best available, and therefore we have to be the number one choice for the kinds of employees we want. After spending time talking with nearly every person we have working at Taylor's, I've outlined the keys to achieving this.

"First and foremost, this has to be a place of integrity, honesty and respect. And that has to begin at the top. We as managers have to do what we say we'll do and treat our people as they would like to be treated. In fact, our goal should be to treat our people as we would like our *customers* to be treated.

"I also believe we should have a system of reward and recognition for employees. I know we've tried this in the past, but we have to make it happen this time. Part of our problem is we have never defined the goal - we just nominate an 'employee of the month,' without ever telling anyone just what that means.

"I recommend we establish specific targets, connected with something we all agree on, like customer service, and provide specific rewards.

Something exciting that will get employees involved in a friendly competition to be the best.

"The atmosphere is also important. Remember, most of these people are part-timers, more often than not kids in school, and kids want to have *fun* - and when you think about it, don't we all? Don't discourage friendships, don't discourage fun. We should even try to create some. That's what will keep people here - most importantly, the outgoing, customer-friendly sort.

"The environment needs to be improved too. This one is tricky because it requires our employees' help. But the cleaner, safer, nicer place we create - the better for everyone. It'll be more enjoyable to work here and we'll attract and retain more customers and employees as well. We need to communicate this to our people, and recognize those employees who follow through."

Then Scott held up a printed poster that read:

Employees First.
Customers Second.

"I know this might strike you as a little off base," Scott said. "But the only ones in a position to treat our customers the way we want them to be treated are our frontline employees. And those employees will treat our customers just as they are treated by us."

Most of Taylor's management staff had come up through the ranks and quickly recognized the truth in what Scott was saying. Even those who hadn't seemed to recognize the common sense it made.

When it came to spending actual money and time on anything, however, management was prone to err on the side of caution and a one-hour debate on the pros and cons ensued. In the end, however, Scott's proposal received management's blessing and the financial support for a six-month trial run for an employee incentive program and half of the funding he wanted for fixing up the work environment.

The next issue Scott had to face was ridding Taylor's of the people with poor attitudes who weren't doing their jobs. Even though it was painful in this short-staffed environment, Scott believed in the long-term they would be better off without the bad influences. He didn't want anyone on board who did not want to be part of a productive team, because bad attitudes affect everyone.

It took some time to get the different aspects of his program off the ground, and not all plans were put into practice perfectly. But as management and employee support grew, Taylor's made several steps forward toward becoming a magnetic company.

CHAPTER 9 HIGHLIGHTS

Plan your work, then work your plan.

Know who you are and what you have to offer.

Never mind what <u>you</u> think! Ask an employee.

*You'll be amazed at what you learn
and begin to achieve "effortlessly"
by simply listening to your employees.*

*The only way to revolutionize recruiting and
hiring is to get management buy-in.*

Employees first. Customers second.

CHAPTER 10:
Attracting Better Applicants

Within a few weeks, Scott felt much better about his recruiting efforts. He knew Taylor's was more appealing as an employer because the number of applicants was increasing.

Everything he'd tried so far had met with success and Scott was excited about Phase Three. Although he was no longer as desperate for people, he still wanted to increase the quality of the applicants who came through the door.

As Scott considered his final touches to his marketing approach to a recruiting system, he spent a minute to take some modest pride in the fact that his store really was a great place to work these days. Even if the increased number of applicants and higher employee satisfaction rankings hadn't told him so, he could see it by just looking around.

Now Scott's goal was to get the word out to as many target applicants as possible and to make it even easier for them to apply.

The first hurdle was the communication itself. While it had evolved from 'Help Wanted' to 'Come Grow with Us,' Scott wanted to further refine the message and also figure out how he could reach people who didn't walk by or come into the store.

So, in line with Tom's advice, Scott interviewed the store's best employees and put together what he called a "lifestyle analysis."

While he found the employees had differing schedules, habits, and hobbies, there were some things most had in common. By trying to recruit people with interests and needs similar to Taylor's best people, Scott hoped to attract more high-caliber candidates.

Use your best employees as sources of research and your standard for new hires.

As it turned out, one of the favorite pastimes of the high school and college students who worked at Taylor's was going to the movies.

"Actually, advertising in movie theaters would be perfect targeted marketing," Scott realized. He called a few local theaters and started making arrangements to produce an on-screen ad to run just before the "Coming Attractions."

Be innovative about where you advertise - go where your target employees go.

While mulling over where else his message might be most effective, Scott struggled with the fact that while classified ads were less and less effective, 87 percent of Taylor's best people read the paper every day - but not necessarily the employment classifieds. In a flash of inspiration, Scott decided it would be worth it to pay a premium and place his recruiting message right next to the movie ads.

> *The newspaper is full of pages your*
> *target applicants read.*
> *The classifieds aren't your only option.*

Because most of Taylor's employee pool was made up of students and retired people, Scott also scheduled time to notify the vocational counselors at the local high schools and get eye-catching signs posted on their campuses.

Then he contacted the local chapter of a nationwide association for retired people to see if he could use their bulletin board and newsletters to get the word out. And, just for good measure, he made up some fliers to post at the local Bingo halls.

"I can't believe I never thought of all these applicant sources before," Scott said to his wife one evening. "I used to think the classifieds were my only tool. Now I have to pick the best, most targeted places to spend my advertising budget. There are so many more options now and I have only so much time and money."

"Tom had a zillion ideas last time I talked to him like putting a recruiting ad on back of our cash register tapes and in the weekly, full page sale ads the store puts in the newspaper every week. He pointed out it wouldn't cost a nickel more to add a recruiting message as standard boilerplate on each and every one. Something like: 'Taylor's - a good place to shop and a good place to work.'

"Community involvement is another great tactic. We could provide free sports drinks for the high school football team and stock them in coolers with Taylor's logo all over them for everyone to see. Then we can encourage coaches and advisors to send kids to Taylor's because we'll work around the students' class and sports schedules too."

Scott thought of more places for recruitment advertising for Taylor's every day. Community centers, neighborhood newsletters, direct mail, the list went on and on. He even got the wheels in motion to add an on-line employment application to Taylor's website.

Target your applicants.
Where do they shop? What do they read? What
do they do for fun?

Next, Scott turned his attention to the message itself. Tom had sent him a copy of an ad a pizza parlor used to attract delivery drivers as an example of an innovative, effective message. The headline read: "Deliver the Pizza, Keep the Dough."

It attracted candidates in an unusual, amusing way, and reinforced the pizza-delivery concept to customers as well. Using that as his model, Scott developed two messages aimed at students and one for retired folks.

He kept the "Come Grow with Us" theme because he knew about 40 percent of the high school students weren't planning on going on to college. For those in school, he settled on: "Nothing's more important than your education. At Taylor's, we'll work around your class schedule."

To attract mature workers, he decided to use the reasons those on staff now told him were appealing: "Some of our best employees are senior citizens. If you'd like to get out of the house, meet new friends, and pick up some mad money, call us today."

Next, Scott decided to make Taylor's even more applicant-friendly. Although great strides had been made, he knew full well that most of the good people who want to work are already working. He had to make it easier for them to apply as well.

"Still not easy enough," Scott decided, after he mentally reviewed the present procedure. "The entire system needs fine tuning, beginning with the application forms."

Make the application process easy.

Scott eyed one of the forms critically. It was passable, but it could certainly look more attractive and he knew it took about 30 minutes, if not longer, for most people to get through it.

He had seen more than one applicant look at the length of the form and then ask if it would be okay to take it home to complete. In order to get a leg up on his competition for hourly employees, Scott knew he had to streamline the process drastically.

When he thought about it, he realized a lot of the information requested was really necessary only if the applicant were actually hired. With the goal of producing a mini-application that could be completed in 10 minutes or less, Scott got out a red pen and started editing.

After about 40 minutes, he was pretty happy with the result. The new form would require only the basics like name, phone number, education, experience, and references. He was about to head for the print shop when he remembered Tom's admonition to not waste time with people who don't have reliable transportation or wouldn't be happy with the wages. He added two questions to cover those bases and headed out the door.

At Speedy Print, he and the typesetter, Sue, talked about jazzing it up with a color logo, better fonts, and high-quality paper. Sue remembered the time she did a cover letter for the owner of the florist shop in their strip mall. Scott's ears perked up as she told him how the owner used it in conjunction with the application.

As she recalled, it briefly covered the application process, a little bit about the business, why hiring the right people was so important to the firm, and thanked the applicants for their time.

Scott thought this addition would really differentiate Taylor's from the competition and told Sue he'd e-mail something like that to her the next day.

"A cover letter would be a good way to let people know Taylor's is only looking for the best of the best," Tom thought while driving. At the next stoplight, he scribbled some notes to remind himself to add a paragraph explaining Taylor's belief that their customers deserve the best and while applying might be easy, only the finest would make the cut. Then he made a note to get the application on the website changed to the new abbreviated version too.

Back at the store the next day, Scott set up a table, two chairs, an upright display of the new applications, a holder full of freshly sharpened pencils, and a slotted application collection box near the main entrance. For the final flourish, he hung a "Come Join Our Team" poster from the ceiling above so it would be easy for applicants to find. He hoped it would also entice some already-employed shoppers to apply too. Now he could accept applications anytime the store was open.

He also sent a memo to all employees to let them know to direct walk-ins to the application station before and after HR hours and how best to field applicant inquiries. He reminded them that while not all applicants would become employees, all were potential customers or could be related to customers and should be extended every courtesy.

While browsing through the employment classifieds the previous Sunday, Scott noticed a number of companies had a toll-free, 24-hour job hotline. When he called the number out of curiosity, he heard an upbeat recruiting message and was walked through a short list of applicant prescreening questions. All he had to do was answer the computerized questions with "1" for "yes" and "2" for "no." Scott could tell by the questions asked that the employer was screening in applicants who met minimum physical and mental capacity requirements.

"Just the ticket for senior citizens and others who might be somewhat interested, but not ready to go to the trouble of coming in," Tom thought.

On Monday, he called one of the local chains he saw in the paper to see what kind of results the hotline was getting. Joe Chang, one of the chain's HR manager said not only were they getting more and better applicants, but also it was saving his store managers a whole lot of time and money. "We were surprised to see how many calls came in during hours our Human Resources Department isn't open. We're getting more good people who already have jobs, but are looking for a change."[1]

*Every interaction with applicants
shapes their impression of your company.
Your ads, your application form, procedures, and
contacts with your employees
are all important. Try to see them from
the applicant's point of view.*

His last adjustment was to change the interview policy so candidates could be interviewed any day and almost any time of the week.

Then Scott called Tom to fill him in on what he'd been up to and told him Taylor's new recruiting philosophy was:

Make the job easy to apply for and hard to get.

"Congratulations, Scott," said Tom. "It sounds like you've made the process simple, pleasant, and

---

[1]Call 1-800-348-0008 to hear a demonstration job hotline. Just follow along with the computerized voice instructions. To learn more you can visit www.humetrics.com.

convenient for most anyone. And making it known you'll only hire the best adds a certain prestige that will naturally attract top quality people and help employee retention too."

From that day on, Scott made sure everyone involved in the recruiting process was kept involved and informed. He made copies of the Job Analysis forms and CAPS model, and held regular training seminars on interviewing skills. Scott now knew Taylor's couldn't afford to make even one bad hire.

CHAPTER 10 HIGHLIGHTS

*Use your best employees as sources of research
and your standard for new hires.*

*Be innovative about where you advertise -
go where your target employees go.*

*The newspaper is full of pages
your target applicants read.
The classifieds aren't your only option.*

*Target your applicants.
Where do they shop? What do they read?
What do they do for fun?*

Make the application process easy.

*Every interaction with applicants shapes their
impression of your company.
Your ads, your application form, procedures, and
contacts with your employees
are all important. Try to see them from the
applicant's point of view.*

Make the job easy to apply for and hard to get.

CHAPTER 11:
Best Sources of Applicants

The next Saturday morning, Scott and Tom met at their favorite golf course at 7:00 a.m. It had rained a little overnight, but by their 7:30 tee time the sun had broken through the few lingering clouds and they could tell it was going to be a great day for chasing little, white, dimpled balls with metal sticks.

The two men had an unspoken agreement not to talk shop until well into their game, but by the fifth hole, Tom could no longer contain his curiosity.

"How's it going at Taylor's these days, Scott?"

"Tom, I owe you big time," Scott exclaimed. "Your marketing approach to recruiting has really worked for us and the unexpected bonus is that I have more time to focus on other things. We're getting more applicants every day."

"Our whole staff seems happier, like more of a team, and we're all more focused on delivering the best customer service in town. You couldn't have been more right. It's a lot easier to get what I need when I *really* know what I'm looking for and where to find it. "

"Are you getting the number of applicants you targeted? And are they of the quality you want?" Tom asked.

"I haven't met my quantity goals yet, but there's a noticeable improvement in quality since we started making it known that not just anybody can get a job at Taylor's."

"Okay, then," said Tom, "now it's time to take a quantum leap. Everything you need to do that is right under your nose."

Scott looked surprised and said, "There's more? I can't imagine. It seems to me I'm already doing everything under the sun."

Tom took a practice swing, lined up over the ball in front of him, and sent it sailing down the fairway. After he completed his swing, he looked at Scott and said, "Your best source of quality applicants is all the good people you have working for you right now."

> *Your current employees are*
> *the best source of new applicants.*

"You know 'the birds of a feather' saying? Well, it holds true when recruiting too. The friends of great people are other great people.

An employee-referral incentive system is one of the most effective recruiting tools you can use."

"You mean reward our staff for recommending their friends?" Scott asked for clarification.

"Yes, exactly," replied Tom. "Usually the way it works is you offer gifts or a prize or, say, $50 or $100 for a referral that leads to a new hire. You pay at least half the award on the new person's first day, and the rest in about three months if they're still with you."

"And don't just tack it onto a paycheck. Create some excitement. Get everyone together and enthusiastically count the amount out into the recipient's hand in small bills. And then milk it for all it's worth. Introduce the new hire by saying something like, 'This is Joe and he's going to be a great cashier because he was recommended to us by Sue, and we all know how great she is.' If you do this, you can take it to the bank that Joe will be doing his best to live up to everyone's high expectations and not let his friend down.

"I've also found there's an immeasurable return on investment when you create a workplace where people can work with their friends.

Although I've heard a horror story now and then, ninety-nine percent of friends working with friends enjoy their jobs more, work better together, and stay on the job longer. In fact, they're the epitome of teamwork.

"Besides, it's *fun* for them, especially the school-age crowd. You said yourself you want to create more fun for the staff. Here's your chance."

"This sounds great," mused Scott, "but I don't have any budget for it. Do you think it would be worth it to dip into my contingency funds?"

"I can promise you, you won't be sorry," Tom replied.

> *An employee referral program is*
> *a cost-effective way*
> *to recruit your employees' friends.*

"And while we're on the subject, what about all the good people who've moved on from Taylor's? Surely you have records on all your former employees. Call up the good ones and ask if they'd like to return."

"But they left for a reason, didn't they? Why would they want to come back?" asked Scott as he knelt to line up his putt.

"They probably left because the grass looked greener elsewhere. They were dissatisfied with something at Taylor's - the pay, their boss, a lack of advancement opportunities - whatever. They believed their problem would disappear when they went elsewhere. But, the truth is, all jobs have problems. If they left for more money, maybe their new boss is a grouch. Or maybe the job isn't what it was cracked up to be. Maybe the place is chaotic and disorganized and the person longs for the ordered and sensible way Taylor's is run. Many people - especially the young ones in first jobs - don't recognize how good they've really got it.

"That's why it's an extremely good use of your time to call the good ones who leave about a month later and see how they're doing. I was religious about this when I was running the restaurants and I'd say 20 percent of the people I called were glad to come back.

"And I knew exactly what I was getting. They knew the business, they were already trained and ready to go.

"The bonus is that, once recruited back, it'll be harder to turn their heads next time a good-looking new job pops up. Plus, they become goodwill ambassadors by telling other employees how good they've got it at Taylor's; this improves retention even more.

"And even if they're happy with their new employer," Tom continued, "they'll be flattered by your offer and probably willing to help you find people. They'll keep you in mind, and suggest Taylor's to friends who are looking for jobs. They may even give you contacts while they're on the phone with you."

"That's another great idea, Tom," Scott exclaimed enthusiastically.

> ***The second best source***
> ***of quality applicants***
> ***is every good employee***
> ***who ever worked for you.***

"There's more," said Tom.

"Why am I not surprised?" asked Scott with a grin.

"Well, I just remembered, and you want to do this right, don't you?" asked Tom. "The thing is you've got to keep detailed contact sheets. Once you've got easily referenced records of referrals, former employees, good applicants you might not have had an opening for at the time they came in, and all your other contacts, you'll be surprised how quickly you can pick up the phone and hire someone."

"Well, Tom, you're certainly on a roll today," said Scott, as he watched Tom's putt for par roll smoothly into the cup. "In this round as well as with the great advice."

"While talking about what's right under our noses - how about your customers?"

Scott interrupted, "Now *that's* something I've thought of myself when I talked to our marketing manager. I saw a little different approach the other day, though. I noticed a sign in a bookstore that read, 'Sometimes Our Customers Make Our Best Employees.'"

"That's it exactly, Scott. In the bookstore's case, it works perfectly. People who like books, who like to read, are natural good fits. They bring a lot of knowledge to the table; they have their love of reading in common with most customers and can make good suggestions. Plus they tend to be happy employees because the environment is to their liking. They have a built-in enthusiasm for the work."

"But can that work for me?" Scott asked dubiously. "I mean, we're a *grocery* store and grocery shopping isn't anyone's favorite pastime."

"It isn't quite as easy, but it's certainly possible. What's extremely likely is some of your customers' kids - the high school or college students - could be just perfect."

Every customer is a source for potential employees.

"Hey, that reminds me," Scott said, "I'd better check on my inventory of grocery bag recruiting inserts. I think I'll look at that again, maybe refine the message even more for the next printing."

"Yes, well, let me also remind you that if you don't sink this putt, you're buying lunch!" Tom crowed.

While Scott was digging his wallet out of his back pocket after lunch, he said to Tom, "I'd gladly buy your lunch every day for the next year, Tom. I don't think you have any idea of how much help you've been to me and to Taylor's."

CHAPTER 11 HIGHLIGHTS

*The best source of applicants
is your current employees.*

*An employee referral program is
a cost-effective way to
recruit the friends of your employees.*

*The second best source of quality applicants is
every good employee who ever worked for you.*

*Every customer is a source of
potential employees.*

CHAPTER 12:
Employee Referral Programs

A couple of weeks later, Katie was cheerfully settled in at Taylor's. Because Old Sourpuss asked nicely, she'd worked at QuickBurger for an additional week while they looked for a replacement and schedules were rearranged.

Life at Taylor's was almost as perfect as she'd dreamed and worlds better than Katie's last job. She was learning new things all the time, and she liked her schedule. Katie's manager had already outlined all the steps necessary in order to get in line for promotion - a welcome change from QuickBurger. She liked having a goal in front of her.

One afternoon, as she stashed her backpack in the employees' locker room, a new sign caught her eye. It read:

Got a friend?
Earn $150!

"What does *that* mean?" Katie asked her new friend Jill, who had worked at Taylor's for three years.

"That's our new Employee Referral Program. It was explained at the monthly staff meeting we had just before you started. They'll probably go over it again at the next one too. A store the size of Taylor's is always looking to hire great people and this program sure helps.

"The idea is you recommend your friends who might be interested as potential employees. If they're a good fit and get hired, you get a $150 cash reward."

"That's it?"

"Yes. Except you get $75 immediately, and the other half three months later if the person is still here. My sister-in-law's employer does this too, but the company is smaller and the award is only $100. She hasn't really participated though because they don't give the money until the new person has been on staff for six whole months. They don't hire tough, like we do here now. She's seen too many people wash out before the employee got the cash."

Katie's mind was buzzing. Why, she knew lots of people. One-hundred-and-fifty dollars for doing practically nothing. She was all in favor of this program.

When she got home from work, her first call that evening was to her old QuickBurger confederate, Derrik.

He sounded pleased to hear from her. "Hey, Kate, what's up? Say, this is perfect timing. You know how I missed the last few days of history class?"

Katie mentally changed gears. "What - oh, right."

"Can I get your notes? Yours are the best," he coaxed.

"Oh, sure," Katie answered, flattered. "I'll bring them tomorrow and you can copy them. But what I called about is do you have any interest in leaving QB and Old Sourpuss? Moving on to better things?"

Her sales pitch was only beginning, but Derrik took the bait right away. "Definitely, yes. Why? Is Taylor's hiring? You like it there?"

"It's great. Everything's better - better schedules, training, promotion opportunities, and you would not believe how many Lincoln High students work there. There are even all sorts of unofficial social events."

"Anyway, we have a program where we recommend friends. I thought I could put your name in, if you like."

"Oh, sure. I'm always into a better job - especially if someone else finds it for me."

"Great. I'll let them know tomorrow."

As Derrik hung up, he congratulated himself on his good fortune. First, he now had history notes - an absolute essential. Mr. Nelson tested on lectures, not reading. And if he didn't pass history, a core course, he would be off the football team.

But all was well now. He had notes - and Kelly's, at that. And maybe a new job too. Derrik didn't much care for the QuickBurger either. He often thought of how he would like to work somewhere better, but never found the time to get out and look.

Later that week, Derrik got a call from Scott's assistant, Ed, who found the high school junior to be outgoing and likeable. After they talked for a few minutes, Ed invited Derrik to Taylor's to fill out an application and to take a short test. If those looked good, he'd have an in-person interview with the big boss, Scott.

Scott was enthusiastic about the possibility of meeting Derrik. Katie was proving to be an excellent hire by all reports, and Scott suspected Derrik would prove to be the same - especially since Ed's initial impression was favorable.

The next day Derrick came in and, after Ed reviewed the required paperwork, was sent upstairs to meet with Scott, who also liked him immediately. "He's easy to talk to and funny," thought Scott, "I know he'd fit right into the group."

Scott did have one reservation though. As far as the mental and physical capacities, personality, and skills went, Derrik was a perfect fit. However, while Derrick had good scores on most all the traits measured by the recently instituted attitude evaluation, his dependability mark was lower than most.

"Tell me Derrick," said Scott, "other than for personal illness, how many times have you missed school or work in the past three months?"

"Gee," said Derrick, scratching his head and looking up. "Maybe six or seven, I really couldn't say for sure."

"And how many times have you been late?"

"Oh, man, that'd be hard to count," puzzled Derrick.

"Amazing what people will tell you," Scott thought.

***Remember, make it easy to apply
and hard to be hired.***

"You simply wouldn't believe all the trouble you've saved me," Scott remarked to Tom over lunch the next day. "Derrik is exactly the sort of person I would have hired immediately four months ago."

Tom agreed with Scott's assessment, but reminded him to be careful in his handling of unsuccessful referrals.

Scott wanted Katie to continue to refer friends, so, in line with Tom's advice, he wrote a personal note...

Katie:

Thank you so much for referring Derrik to us. I found him to be very likeable. Unfortunately, none of the positions we have open right now would be a perfect fit for him and you know how hard we work to put the right person in the right position.

Thanks again for the referral and please continue to bring any potential candidates to our attention.

Sincerely, Scott Miller

Handling Derrik was more challenging. Ordinarily, Scott would simply have his assistant fire off a thanks-but-no-thanks form letter. In this case, however, Scott felt Taylor's had essentially *invited* Derrik to apply, then refused him. Tom's advice still rang in Scott's head:

Every applicant is a potential customer.

Scott decided to err on the side of tact. He wrote a personal letter in the same vein, thanked Derrik for his time and encouraged him to consider Taylor's in the future. Scott then put both notes in the outgoing mail tray.

Three days later, the day after Katie and Derrik got the notes from Scott, Derrik seemed unruffled when Katie talked to him in history class.

"You never know, it was worth a try," Derrik said, making it clear he thought of the hiring process as an unfathomable mystery. "Thanks anyway, I did get a nice note from Scott. Say, do you happen to have your English notes from yesterday?"

Katie was glad Taylor's had been so nice to Derrik and that he wasn't angry. She did miss working with him though, she reflected. But, on second thought, she would not really miss covering for him and concluded everything had worked out for the best.

CHAPTER 12 HIGHLIGHTS

Employee referral programs work.

*Remember, make it easy to apply
and hard to be hired.*

Every applicant is a potential customer.

CHAPTER 13: Managing Turnover

A few days after Tom and his wife returned from an extended golf vacation, Tom decided to drop by Taylor's to check in with Scott and see how things were going. As he made his way back to Scott's office, he took time to get a feel for how things had progressed.

There was not much to criticize. The store appeared to be fully staffed and it was cleaner, brighter, and more alive than he remembered.

Scott was just ending an interview in the lobby when he noticed Tom heading his way. After he shook hands with the applicant and sent her on her way, he called out to Tom, "Hey, buddy. What a nice surprise."

"Saturday morning interviews, huh, pal?" Tom laughed, as he followed Scott back to his office.

"You bet," Scott grinned, "turns out it's the most convenient time for school kids. What brings you here?"

"Well, I've been gone over a month and was curious to find out how things are going."

"You'd be amazed," Scott said. "I'm continually adding staff because we keep getting more and more customers. Sales are way up. It hasn't been a problem though because we've had a steady stream of qualified applicants for the past two months. You wouldn't believe how busy it is around here."

"Oh, yes, I would. You've become a *magnetic company*! Now you're so busy being successful, you've no time for anything else."

"Well, I'm not too busy to buy you lunch," laughed Scott, as he turned Tom by the shoulders and gently pushed him toward the door.

Over lunch, Scott described Taylor's success.

"It's like that dream I had in the park," he enthused. "It's as good as we ever hoped - and it's only a few months since I first came to you for advice.

"John is happy, Donna Romano is happy - and so am I. The icing on the cake is I was given a 15 percent raise yesterday.

Scott continued thoughtfully, "And all the people I talk to at our Chamber of Commerce meetings are still desperately trying to hire anyone who passes a pulse test while I get to pick the best of the best. Our competition thinks we're paying more, but we haven't had to."

"Well, if you're enjoying that much success, maybe I should take this course on the road," observed Tom. "I could make an awful lot of money..."

"Don't do that," Scott interjected. "I'm enjoying this advantage. I like being the only *magnetic company* in town."

"Okay, okay, my lips are sealed as far as your competition goes, but I've got to warn you, I've got quite a few bright business majors in my classes who will be out in your world in a couple of years. So you'd better stay on your toes."

"You can bet I will," said Scott. "Anything you've told them you haven't told me yet?"

"Well, let me think for a minute," said Tom. "Ah, yes. Do you remember when we talked about the objective being to manage turnover, rather than trying to eliminate it?"

"Like it was yesterday," said Scott.

"This philosophy is very important for you now that you've got a successful program up and running. Now you're in what I call maintenance mode.

"You should always be looking for your next employee and have people waiting in the wings, so to speak, for when you promote from within, or someone leaves for college, or an employee's spouse is transferred. The best time to look for any employee is when you don't need one. You needn't hire anyone if you don't need to - you just need to continually recruit and interview. Then, when someone quits, you're not starting at square one.

The best time to look for your next employee is before you need one.

"You will need to make an exception every once in while, however. If someone absolutely perfect shows up, someone who easily passes all your pre-screening and gets glowing references, you probably shouldn't let that person get away. If you can, create a spot for them. You'd hate to lose them to the competition.

"And plan for your peak seasons. You know when they are - as does everyone in retail. Yet think how many don't start looking for Christmas help until almost Thanksgiving.

"Inevitably most are left short-handed. What if they had started searching two months earlier? Sure, they may have run up the budget a little - but think how many more applicants they'd have to choose from. They could avoid desperation hiring and have a good chance of being able to deliver quality customer service during their peak season.

Plan and hire for seasonal fluctuations in advance.

"When managing turnover, be sure to track the difference between natural turnover and artificial turnover. Artificial turnover results from poor hiring decisions, bad management, and unhappy employees. Artificial turnover is extremely destructive and it tends to spiral higher and higher. By tracking it, you can nip problems in the bud.

"Natural turnover is when the straight-A student you hired goes off to college or the ambitious, young worker gets promoted. It's what's *going* to happen - in part, because things change, and, in part, because you're hiring the kind of people who don't stay in one place for long."

"You mean good people will always want to leave, and that's supposed to be a good thing?"

"Some good people will leave, yes. Your job is to process them through Taylor's so they leave their old jobs, but stay on at the company. You'll still have to replace the cashier, for example, if you promote her.

"But you'll *keep* her, and you won't need to look for an experienced, knowledgeable assistant manager. And if you hadn't promoted her, you'd have lost her. All because you hired a promotable person in the first place.

"The key, then, is to be proactive. Hire the best and do whatever it takes to keep them. Don't hold them back."

"That *is* an important concept," Scott agreed. "All right, I'm with you. But as I continue to recruit, do I use the same strategy I've been using?"

"You can lighten up a bit as you've got the natural attraction of being a *magnetic company* working for you now. I know your early stage was expensive. Now think of your recruiting budget like a series of ocean waves."

"Like *what*? Where do you get these analogies?"

"Think of the natural pattern of the waves at an ocean beach. One big one, three or four small ones, then another big one. Recruit using this rhythm. Make a big splash for a couple of weeks, then run three or four smaller campaigns. Just always keep your message out there. New people are always moving here and employed people get fed up with their jobs every day. By keeping your name out there, you're less likely to miss any opportunities.

Stick with a sustained recruiting effort of varying intensity.

"And remember, your competition for employees is not only other grocers, but any business or organization where the kind of person you want to hire can be employed.

"Congratulations, Scott. You've done the hard part the rest is just keeping your head down and your eye on the ball. Do you know how few companies and managers use these principles or even think about them? You deserve to enjoy every moment of the competitive advantage you've created - Taylor's is now a *MAGNETIC COMPANY! "*

CHAPTER 13 HIGHLIGHTS

*You can't eliminate turnover,
but you can manage it.*

*The best time to look for your next employee is
before you need one.*

*Plan and hire for
seasonal fluctuations in advance.*

*Stick with a sustained recruiting effort
of varying intensity.*

CHAPTER 14:
Magnetic Companies
Create Win/Win Situations

The next Wednesday, Katie and Becky sat in the school's outside courtyard having lunch. Again the duo was eagerly looking forward to a game on Friday, and all that stood between them and the game were their Wednesday and Thursday afternoon shifts and two-and-a-half days of school. They were both still happy with their jobs - as happy as teens can get about any kind of work anyway.

Katie leaned back against a tree and started opening her candy bar. "What amazes me is how long it took me to dump QuickBurger for Taylor's."

"What amazes me is how, on day two at Taylor's, you met Todd, and, by day four, you were practically engaged," Becky tossed back.

"I know you like your job, Becky, but think about what you're missing. You're never gonna meet any guys in a women's clothing store. Taylor's is so full of cool guys, I'd work there for free."

"I hope you haven't told your manager that," Becky intoned with mock gravity. "You do have a point though. As much as I like Remington's, I haven't seen a guy my age in there since last Christmas."

"If you want me to put your name in at Taylor's, I'll split the referral bonus with you," Katie offered.

"Thanks, but I'm still mostly happy where I am except for the fact my schedule is creeping up in hours."

"Better make sure you tell them," Katie warned. Having held *two* jobs, Katie was now the expert on employment matters for the pair.

The girls didn't talk again until almost ten o'clock that evening. When Katie got home from work, she found four messages from Becky on her answering machine. She didn't sound any too happy, either.

Wondering what on earth was going on, Katie called her right back.

"You won't believe this," Becky said near tears. "Remington's wants me to work Friday night until 1:00 a.m."

"What? One a.m.? Why? It - it's the big game. We'd planned…"

"I know, I know, but it's the Round-the-Clock Sale. The mall is open until midnight."

"But I thought…"

"Oh, I was supposed to have it off. I cleared it weeks ago. But Rachel wants it off - some college party has come up."

"But you had it first," Katie reminded her.

"Like that matters," Becky interrupted bitterly. "Don't forget - Rachel has *seniority*. Seniority, my foot. They wouldn't let anyone else get away with this. It's because she's the owner's niece, that's all. My life is ruined."

> *Don't try to guess what's of critical importance to your employees.*
> *You'll never get it right.*
> *You've got to ask them.*

"But didn't you say something?" Katie asked sympathetically.

"Naturally. It turned into a blowout, too. I left in tears, but my manager still said I've got no choice."

"Well, of all the nasty tricks, springing this on you at the last minute," summed up Katie. "Wait, I know. Call Taylor's 24-hour job hotline and don't forget to say I referred you. Then you can call Remington's and tell them you have a new job, thank you. That'll show them."

Becky paused. "Do you think they would hire me?"

"Oh, yes," Katie exclaimed. "Call tonight and get yourself in the system. Maybe Taylor's can be the answer."

Becky insisted they hang up that minute. "I'm going to call now," she said, "while I'm still good and mad."

> *Many hourly employees leave jobs*
> *because of a conflict with the*
> *manager over a scheduling issue.*

Becky called the toll-free number and punched in a remarkable amount of information about herself considering it was all accomplished with a telephone keypad.

She went to bed that evening with a sliver of hope. She couldn't afford to go unemployed - but maybe Taylor's would hire her. Then she could go to the big game after all.

Thursday morning before school, Katie visited Scott personally to plead Becky's case. But it really wasn't necessary - the 24-hour job hotline had already identified Becky as a prime candidate, and she was on Scott's "to call" list. After he chatted with Katie for a minute and got some background, he asked Katie to ask Becky to drop by his office after school that day.

Becky went to Taylor's right from school and breezed through the pre-screen and attitude evaluation. She was clearly an enthusiastic and intelligent young woman, and by the end of the interview Scott had no doubts about her. The reference check calls Ed made to a couple of her teachers while Scott and Becky talked verified his impressions.

"Well, Becky, I'm very pleased to offer you a job here at Taylor's."

She was happy and shocked at the same time. This had all happened so fast. Taylor's had made it so easy.

Scott caught her facial expressions as she reacted to the offer and silently thanked Tom for stressing the advantages of rapid hiring procedures. Scott had a feeling Becky was just one of many he could win over when the time was right. And employees like her didn't come along every day - you had to catch them when you could.

***Sometimes the best way to attract a candidate
who is not seeking employment
is to let them in during a moment
of unhappiness with their current employer.
The key to this strategy is quick action.***

Becky had one concern though and, before officially accepting, said, "My biggest problem with Remington's, Scott, is the scheduling. They can't seem to come up with something predictable for me at the 20-hour-per-week level. Can Taylor's?"

In his earlier research, Scott had learned that the frontline employees had an inside joke about flexible hours. They'd kid around that the term meant the employee had to be flexible enough to work wherever and whenever the employer wanted.

Scott was working to correct that problem and promised Becky a maximum of 20 hours per week on a fixed schedule. Knowing Katie had the same arrangement, Becky didn't doubt Scott would keep his word.

> ***The key to success is
> to meet your applicant's needs.
> Do whatever it takes
> to make it a win/win situation.***

Becky thought for a few more minutes. She didn't want to rush into anything, even to be able to go to the game that night. But Scott was so pleasant and was offering her the same money plus a predictable, agreeable schedule. And Katie worked here, too - and so did all those guys. What was she waiting for?

Becky accepted. On her way to Remington's to give notice, she wondered if it would mean Rachael couldn't go to her party after all. She couldn't help but smile to herself when she thought of this prospect. It was about time Rachael got back what she was always dishing out!

CHAPTER 14 HIGHLIGHTS

*Don't try to guess what's of
critical importance to your employees.
You'll never get it right.
You've got to ask them.*

*Many hourly employees leave job
because of a conflict with the
manager over a scheduling issue.*

*Sometimes the best way to attract a candidate
who is not seeking employment is to let them in
during a moment of unhappiness
with their current employer. The key to this
strategy is quick action.*

*The key to success is to
meet your applicant's needs.
Do whatever it takes to make it a
win/win situation.*

FREE NEWSLETTER:

*If you liked this book, you'll love our free,
monthly, e-mail newsletter. It's packed with
hourly employee recruiting, selection, and
retention news you can use!*

To subscribe, visit: http://www.hiretough.com

APPENDIX

Recruit Smarter Philosophy

☑ Take a marketing approach to recruiting.

☑ Happy employees make customers happy. Happy customers make management happy

☑ Keeping the good employees you have happy is just as important as attracting new ones.

☑ Great employees are out there and they usually work for great companies. Traditional recruiting methods will never reach them.

☑ If you don't know what - or whom - you're looking for, you'll never find it.

☑ Not all employees are inspired by the same motivators.

☑ While running a business is serious, there's no reason it can't be fun.

☑ Great employees are invaluable. The time and money it takes to find them generate a huge return-on-investment.

☑ To be the best, you must hire the best. To hire the best, you must recruit the best because the best you can hire is no better than the best of those who apply.

☑ Insanity: Doing the same thing over and over again and expecting a different result!

☑ Hourly employees are unlikely to tolerate a disagreeable situation for long.

☑ There are lots of jobs available - and every applicant knows it.

☑ A company does not attract the best by accident.

☑ If you're serious about recruiting great people, you have to be serious about your process.

☑ To screen-in the best, make it easy to apply, but hard to get hired.

☑ You can't eliminate turnover, but you can manage it.

☑ Employees first. Customers second.

Recruit Smarter Tactics

☑ Looking for an employee without knowing what you need is like grocery shopping without a list. Write your job analysis.

☑ Know the difference between what you need to have and what would be nice to have.

☑ Hiring is not always the answer. Look for alternatives to hiring a new, permanent, full-time worker. Automation and technology may be cost-efficient and eliminate the need for a position.

☑ Exit interviews and surveys of former employees are excellent sources of information.

☑ Use your best employees as sources of research and your standard for new hires.

☑ Leverage your marketing and recruiting efforts off of each other.

☑ Market to the centers of influence (parents, teachers, peers, etc.) as well as to your target recruits.

☑ Project a positive image. Potential recruits are attracted by image, not reality. Create an environment that attracts the best employees naturally; don't rely on gimmicks and advertisements.

☑ Know who you are and what you have to offer.

☑ It's essential to differentiate yourself, especially in challenging hiring markets.

☑ Think of positive, creative ways to replace "Now Hiring" and "Help Wanted" signs. Use creative messages and signs to differentiate yourself from your competition.

☑ You can't train someone to smile or be dependable, so identifying the right attitudes is essential. Ask the right questions or buy validated attitude testing from a reliable vendor because the number-one reason to hire or fire an hourly employee is *attitude*.

☑ Personality and attitudes are much more than just "click." Look for the person who is best for the job - not the person you like best.

☑ Never hire someone you wouldn't hire if you weren't desperate.

☑ The applicant's initial experience is critical. Frontline staff needs to understand the importance and etiquette of recruiting.

☑ Making a great impression may not be enough. If your process is too slow, you may lose applicants to faster competitors. Look for ways to speed things up.

☑ Develop a system that uses more of the applicant's time and less of yours.

☑ Never mind what you think they want or need. Ask your employees. You'll be amazed at what you learn and begin to achieve "effortlessly" - by simply listening.

☑ Get management buy-in.

☑ Be innovative about where you advertise - go where your target employees go.

☑ The newspaper is full of pages your target applicants read. The classifieds aren't your only option.

☑ Target your applicants. Where do they shop? What do they read? What do they do for fun?

☑ Every interaction with applicants shapes their impression of your company. Your ads, your application form and process, and contacts with your employees are all important. Try to see them from the applicant's point of view.

☑ Make the job easy to apply for and hard to get.

☑ The best source of applicants is your current employees. An employee referral program is a cost-effective way to recruit your employees' friends.

☑ The second best source of quality applicants is every good employee who ever worked for you. Call them.

☑ Every customer is a source of potential employees. Get the message out.

☑ Treat every applicant as a potential customer.

☑ Plan and hire for seasonal fluctuations in advance.

☑ Stick with a sustained recruiting effort of varying intensity.

☑ Don't try to guess what's of critical importance to your employees. You'll never get it right. You've got to ask them.

☑ Many hourly employees leave jobs because of a conflict with the manager over a scheduling issue. Don't make this mistake.

☑ Sometimes the best way to attract a candidate who is not seeking employment is to let them in during a moment of unhappiness with their current employer. The key to this strategy is quick action.

☑ The key to success is to meet your applicant's needs. Do whatever it takes to create a win/win situation.

About the HIRE TOUGH Group

More than 70 percent of all U.S. wages and salaries go to hourly workers, yet little attention is paid to how these employees are recruited, selected, and retained. HIRE TOUGH is devoted to these issues. We understand the unique challenges faced by organizations that rely on hourly employees and offer proven solutions that will help you attract and select the best employees.

The HIRE TOUGH system for recruiting and selecting hourly employees is being used by thousands of companies across the U.S. The HIRE TOUGH fundamental principle is simple, yet powerful -- hiring the right employee the first time will reduce turnover.

The HIRE TOUGH Group provides a complete resource of information, training workshops, consulting services, tools, and publications all centered on the HIRE TOUGH philosophy.

For more information, call 1.877.447.3868 or visit us on the web at www.hiretough.com.

About HUMETRICS

For more than 25 years, Humetrics has been helping thousands of companies address the challenges of finding and screening the best hourly employees. Humetrics compliments a company's existing hiring system with an automated application process that combines telephone job hotlines, in-store kiosks, corporate Websites and Internet job boards. Humetrics can continue to support employers through the hiring process by helping companies with validated testing and background checks,

Welfare Opportunity Tax Credits (WOTC), W-2s, I-9s, and in-depth reporting.

To learn more about Humetrics visit us on the web at www.humetrics.com or call 1-800-627-HIRE.

Help your company

RECRUIT SMARTER, NOT HARDER

For information on multiple-copy book orders, live training workshops and products call 877.447.3868 or visit www.hiretough.com.